Table of Conte

1. Sequence And Series..................................
2. Quadratic Equations...12
3. Counting Principles...20
4. Mathematical Induction..24
5. Binomial Expansion...29
6. Polynomials...33
7. Complex Numbers...41
8. Circular Functions and Trigonometry...48
9. Functions..65
10. Vectors..76
11. Limits and Differentiation..93
12. Integration...109
13. Statistics and Probability..116
14. Answers 124

Preface

This revision guide can be used by anyone prepping for Pre-University Mathematics exams but it has been tailored to the International baccalaureate syllabus of 2014. The book explains mathematical concepts laconically and helps those students who are doing a final revision right before they take their exam. The questions at the end of each chapter are similar to those you will finally face and thus practising them would reinforce the concepts learnt before.

Mathematics is not a hard subject at all. For starters there are no words and thus your answers will not depend on what the examiner makes of it. The answers are definite and there are many ways of getting to it, some of which are explained in this book. There is nothing that needs to be memorised in order to answer a mathematics question. Only the thorough understanding on mathematical concepts is paramount.

I thank my tutor Mr Rajdeep Ghai for his wisdom and support and Mr Amit Sharma for making sure the book does not contain any errors

To my parents Pradeep and Rekha for believing in me

SEQUENCES AND SERIES

1.1 Arithmetic sequences and series;
   - sum of finite arithmetic series;
   Geometric sequences and series;

   - Sum of finite and infinite geometric series.
   Sigma notation.

Concepts

- A sequence is an ordered list of numbers defined by a rule
- The numbers in a sequence are its 'terms'.
- An infinite sequence continues indefinitely. for example: 1,2,3,4 ....
- A finite sequence is a sequence that terminates.
- Formula that represents the nth term is called the 'general term'. $u_n = n + 1$ is the general term of the sequence 1,2,3,4 ....

Arithmetic sequences

Definition - Each term differs from the previous by the same fixed number. And this fixed number is called the **common difference** denoted by the letter 'd'. u_1 is the **first term** of the sequence and u_n is the **general term**.

Some basic properties that can be used to save time are:

If u_{n-1}, u_n, and u_{n+1} are terms of an arithmetic sequence

- $u_{n+1} - u_n = u_n - u_{n-1}$
- $2u_n = u_{n+1} + u_{n-1}$
- $U_n = \frac{u_{n+1} + u_{n-1}}{2}$

The general term of an arithmetic sequence is given by

$u_n = u_1 + (n-1)d$, where n is the term that you want to find. Although u_1 is used to denote the first term of the sequence, the letter a is used on the exam.

Arithmetic series

A series is a set of numbers that have a '+' symbol in between each term. For e.g. A **sequence** would be 1, 4, 7, 10, 13 etc. but a **series** would be the sum of the terms in a sequence $1 + 4 + 7 + 10 + 13$ etc.

The general formula to find the sum of 'n' terms of a series is given by:

$$S_n = \frac{n}{2}((2 \times u_1) + (n-1)d)$$

But if the first term(u_1) of the sequence and the nth term of the sequence(u_n) is given to you then the sum of n terms of the sequence can be found using:

$$S_n = \frac{n}{2}(u_1 + u_n)$$

Solved example:

- In the arithmetic series with n^{th} term u_n, it is given that $u_3 = 9$ and $u_7 = 17$. Find the minimum value of n so that $u_1 + u_2 + u_3 + \ldots + u_n > 4500$.

So using the equation for the general term of the sequence we know:

$$u_3 = u_1 + (3-1)d$$

Or since we know the value of u_3

$$9 = u_1 + (2)d \quad\text{———}\quad \text{①}$$

And for u_7

$$u_7 = u_1 + (7-1)d$$

This can be written as

$$17 = u_1 + (6)d \quad\text{———}\quad \text{②}$$

We now have simultaneous equations which we can use to solve for u_1 and for d. This can then be used to solve for the sum of the series to find the minimum value of n.

$$9 = u_1 + (2)d$$

$$17 = u_1 + (6)d$$

$$-8 = -4d$$

$$d = 2 \quad and \quad u_1 = 5$$

Now the equation for the sum of a series is

$$S_n = \frac{n}{2}((2 \times u_1) + (n-1)d)$$

We know that we need to find the value of n for which

$$\frac{n}{2}((2 \times 5) + (n-1) \times 2) > 4500$$

Solve the inequality to get

$$\frac{n}{2}(10 + 2n - 2) > 4500$$

$$\frac{n}{2}(8 + 2n) > 4500$$

$$n(8 + 2n) > 9000$$

$$8n + 2n^2 > 9000$$

$$2n^2 + 8n - 9000 > 0$$

Solving this will give you $n > 65.11$

And since the nth term can't be a decimal value look for the next whole number which is 66. So the minimum value for n such that $u_1 + u_2 + u_3 + \ldots + u_n > 4500$ is 66.

Geometric sequences

Definition- Each term is obtained from the previous by multiplying it by the same non-zero constant. $\{u_n\}$ is geometric if $\frac{u_{n+1}}{u_n} = r$ for $n \in Z^+$ where 'r' is a constant common ratio.

All other terminology are the same for a geometric sequence as they were for an arithmetic sequence.

Some basic properties that can be used to save time are

If u_{n-1}, u_n, and u_{n+1} are terms of a geometric sequence,

$$\frac{u_n}{u_{n-1}} = \frac{u_{n+1}}{u_n}$$

$$u_n^2 = (u_{n+1})(u_{n-1})$$

$$u_n = \pm\sqrt{(u_{n+1})(u_{n-1})}$$

The general term of a geometric sequence is given by

$u_n = u_1 \times r^{(n-1)}$, where n is the term that you want to find.

Geometric series

It is the sum of terms in a geometric sequence

The general formula to find the sum of 'n' terms of a series is given by:

$$S_n = \frac{u_1(r^n - 1)}{r - 1} \text{ if } r > 1 \quad \text{or} \quad \frac{u_1(1 - r^n)}{1 - r} \text{ if } r < 1$$

New ideas in a geometric series

Convergent series

- if $|r| < 1$
- as n becomes large, $r^n \to 0$
- As n becomes large. $S_n = \frac{u_1}{1-r}$

Divergent series:

1. if $|r| > 1$
    - the sum is infinitely large

On the examination if you are asked to find out or prove that a series is convergent or divergent just check whether |r|<1 or |r|>1 respectively

Solved example:

- A geometric sequence $u_1, u_2, u_3, \ldots$ has $u_1 = 14$ and a sum to infinity of 42. Find the common ratio of the geometric sequence.

We know that to find the sum to infinity we use the formula: $\frac{u_1}{1-r}$. In this question we are given u_1 and the sum to infinity.

$$\frac{14}{1-r} = 42$$

$$\frac{14}{42} = 1 - r$$

$$\frac{1}{3} = 1 - r$$

$$r = 1 - \frac{1}{3}$$

$$r = \frac{2}{3}$$

The sum of the first two terms of a geometric series is $\frac{9}{2}$ and the sum of its first 4 terms is $\frac{45}{8}$. Find the first term and the common ratio if the common ratio is positive.

the general term of any sequence is given by:

$u_n = a \times r^{(n-1)}$ Where a is the first term of the sequence as mentioned before.

So it is given in the question that

$$a + (a \times r^{2-1}) = \frac{9}{2}$$

$$a + (r \times a) = \frac{9}{2}$$

$$a(1 + r) = \frac{9}{2} \longrightarrow \text{hence } (1 + r) \text{ can be written as } \frac{9}{2a}$$

$$a + ar = \frac{9}{2}$$

And that the sum of 4 terms is $\frac{45}{8}$, which can be expressed as:

$$a + ar + ar^2 + ar^3 = \frac{45}{8}$$

$$\frac{9}{2} + ar^2(1 + r) = \frac{45}{8}$$

$$\frac{9}{2} + \cancel{a}r^2 \left(\frac{9}{2\cancel{a}}\right) = \frac{45}{8}$$

$$\frac{9}{2} + \frac{9}{2}r^2 = \frac{45}{8}$$

$$\frac{9 + 9r^2}{2} = \frac{45}{8}$$

$$9 + 9r^2 = \frac{\cancel{45}}{\cancel{8}_4} \times \cancel{2}$$

$$9 + 9r^2 = \frac{45}{4}$$

$$4(9 + 9r^2) = 45$$

$$36 + 36r^2 = 45$$

$$36r^2 = 9$$

$$r^2 = \frac{9}{36} = \frac{1}{4}$$

$$r = \frac{1}{2}$$

$$1 + \frac{1}{2} = \frac{9}{2a}$$

$$\frac{3}{2} = \frac{9}{2a}$$

$6a = 18$

$a = 3$

Sigma notation

This just means the sum of numbers. The symbol Σ is used to denote sigma. The sigma symbol is always followed by a general term of an arithmetic sequence.

There are a few properties of sigma notation that must be remembered:

$$\sum_{i=1}^{n}[u_i + v_i] = \sum_{i=1}^{n} u_i + \sum_{i=1}^{n} v_i$$

$$\sum_{i=1}^{n} ku_i = k \sum_{i=1}^{n} u_i$$

$$\sum_{i=1}^{n} k = kn$$

Where k is a constant

Solved example:

$$- find \sum_{i=1}^{5} n + 1$$

So in this case, if the question arises on the non-calculator paper, you will have to do the summation manually.

Since n starts from 1 in this question, the first 5 terms would be 1,2,3,4,5

And the sum of these numbers would be $1 + 2 + 3 + 4 + 5 = 15$

Practice time!

1. A geometric sequence has a first term 7 and a sum to infinity of 28. Find the common ratio.
2. In an arithmetic sequence (general term u_n) $u_3 = 17$ and $u_{10} = 52$. Find the minimum value of n for which the sum of the terms in the sequence is > 5500.
3. Deduce from the arithmetic sequence $9, 14, 19, 24 \ldots$
   a. The nth term of the sequence
   b. The sum of the first 68 terms
4. The average of the first 10 terms of an arithmetic sequence is $\frac{31}{2}$ and the average of the first 17 terms is 26. What is the 4th term in this sequence?
5. The sum of the first 4 terms of a geometric sequence is 40 and that of the first 7 terms is 1093. Find the first term and the common ratio.
6. The common ratio of a geometric sequence is 1.2^x. Find the values of x for which the sum to infinity of the sequence does NOT exist.
7. A geometric sequence has a first term 3.5 and a common ratio of 2.3. Find the value of the smallest term greater than 375.
8. A ball bounces from a height of 6 meters and returns to 78% of its previous height on each bounce. Find the total distance travelled by the ball.
9. Deduce from the geometric sequence, $25, 15, 9, \frac{27}{5} \ldots$ Which term of the sequence is 0.0327.
10. Calculate the number of terms in the geometric sequence $14, 7, 3.5 \ldots \frac{7}{262144}$.
11. Annie invests $3000 in the bank at an interest of 3.2% p.a. How much money will she have at the end of 8 years if
    a. The interest is compounded monthly
    b. If the interest is compounded half yearly
12. How much will frank have at the end of 15 years if his initial amount invested was $6700 at a rate of 5.6% p.a. compounded half yearly?

QUADRATIC EQUATIONS

2.6   Solving quadratic equations using the quadratic formula.
Use of the discriminant $\Delta = b^2 - 4ac$ to determine the nature of the roots.
May be referred to as roots of equations or zeros of functions.
Solving polynomial equations both graphically and algebraically.
Sum and product of the roots of polynomial equations.

<u>Quadratic equation:</u> $ax^2 + bx + c\,; a, b, c\ are\ constants\,; a \neq 0$

<u>Quadratic function:</u> $y = f(x) = ax^2 + bx + c\,; a \neq 0$

Solutions

The values of 'x' for which the equation $ax^2 + bx + c = 0$ *is true*

These solutions (also known as roots) are the x-intercepts of a graph of a quadratic function $f(x) = ax^2 + bx + c$.

There are different ways to solve a quadratic equation

  – **Factorization**

Solved example:

$x^2 - 2x = 15$

1. $x^2 - 2x - 15 = 0$ → Rearrange the equation so all the terms are on one side and it is equated 0

2. $x^2 - 3x + 5x - 15 = 0$

   $x(x - 3) + 5(x - 3) = 0$ → Factorisation

   $(x + 5)(x - 3) = 0$

3. $(x + 5) = 0\ or$

   $(x - 3) = 0$ → Use the idea that if $\times q = 0$, then $p = 0$ or $q = 0$

   $x = -5, x = 3$

- **Completing the squares**

Solved example:

$$x^2 + 4x + 1 = 0$$

Recognize that the quadratic equation above is not a perfect square, e.g. $(x + 2)^2 = x^2 + 4x + 4$. So it can be written as:

1. $x^2 + 4x + 4 - 3 = 0$

   $(x + 2)^2 - 3 = 0$

   → Convert the form $ax^2 + bx + c = 0$ into $a(x - h)^2 + k = 0$

2. $(x + 2)^2 = 3$

   $x + 2 = \pm\sqrt{3}$

   → Factorise and then solve for x

   $\therefore x = -2 + \sqrt{3}$,

   $x = -2 - \sqrt{3}$

- **Graphical method**

Solved example:

Plot the graph using a graphing calculator and then see where the graph cuts the x-axis. Either both roots of the quadratic function would be real or they would both be imaginary.

$$x^2 - 4x - 5 = 0$$

$$\therefore f(x) = x^2 - 4x - 5$$

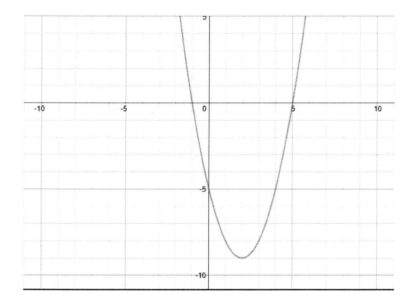

- **Use the quadratic formula**

$x = \frac{-b \pm \sqrt{b^2 - 4ac}}{2a}$ where the letters in the formula correspond to the letters in the general form of a quadratic equation which is $ax^2 + bx + c$.

Solved example

$3x^2 - x - 1 = 0$

$a = 3$

$b = -1$

$c = -1$

$x = \frac{1 \pm \sqrt{(-1)^2 - 4(3)(-1)}}{2(3)}$

$$x = \frac{1+\sqrt{13}}{6}; x = \frac{1-\sqrt{13}}{6}$$

Discriminant (Δ)

1. $\Delta = b^2 - 4ac$
2. *can be used to determine the nature of the roots of a quadratic equation*

Discriminant value	Nature of roots	Graph
$\Delta > 0$	2 distinct real roots	Intersects x-axis at 2 distinct points
$\Delta = 0$	2 identical real roots	touches x-axis at 1 point
$\Delta < 0$	No real roots (cannot factorise)	Does not intersect the x-axis (i.e. above or below)

Sum and Product of Roots

- *can be used to find out the coefficients of a quadratic equation when given the roots*

Let the roots of quadratic equation $ax^2 + bx + c = 0$ be α and β.

$$ax^2 + bx + c = a(x - \alpha)(x - \beta)$$
$$= a(x^2 - \alpha x - \beta x + \alpha\beta)$$
$$= a(x^2 - (\alpha + \beta)x + \alpha\beta)$$

so, $x^2 + \frac{b}{a}x + \frac{c}{a} = x^2 - (\alpha + \beta)x + \alpha\beta$

Equating coefficients: $\alpha + \beta = \frac{-b}{a}$ and $\alpha\beta = \frac{c}{a}$

Graphs

- The graph of a quadratic function $f(x) = ax^2 + bx + c$ is called a parabola
- A graph with a minimum turning point is 'concave upward' and with a maximum turning point is 'concave downward'. If the equation is $-ax^2 + bx + c$ then the graph has a maximum point. If the equation is $ax^2 + bx + c$ then there is a minimum point.
- A graph can be used to find out the equation of the quadratic function

On the exam the quadratic function may be represented in different ways but the questions remain the same

If the quadratic function is of the form

$$y = ax^2 + bx + c$$

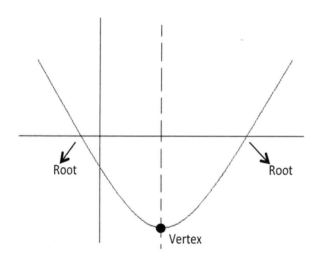

The $y - intercept$ is given by c

Axis of symmetry about which the graph of a quadratic function is symmetrical is given by:

$$x = \frac{-b}{2a}$$

The coordinates of the vertex is given by $\left(\frac{-b}{2a}, c - \frac{b^2}{4a}\right)$

Roots when the discriminant $\Delta \geq 0$ is given by $x = \frac{-b \pm \sqrt{b^2 - 4ac}}{2a}$

$y = a(x - p)(x - q)$

Axis of symmetry: $x = \frac{p+q}{2}$

The coordinates of the vertex $\left(\frac{p+q}{2}, f(\frac{p+q}{2})\right)$

Roots = p and q

$y = a(x - p)^2$

Axis of symmetry: $x = p$

The coordinates of the vertex $(p, 0)$

Root = p ($\Delta = 0$) which means that this equation only has one root. So the graph just touches the x-axis at one point.

$y = a(x - p)^2 + q$

Axis of symmetry: $x = p$

The coordinates of the vertex (p, q)

The graph will not intersect $x - axis$, if $\Delta < 0$. So no real roots.

Point(s) of intersection between a linear function and a quadratic function

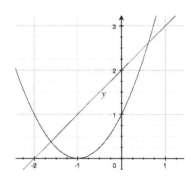 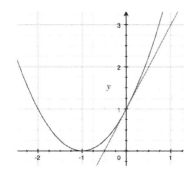 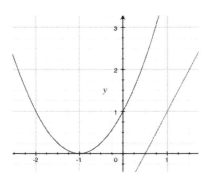

So the three cases shown above are the line and the curve cuts at two places, one place or no intersection point at all.

Solved example

Find the coordinates of the points of intersection of the graphs with equations $f(x) = x^2 + 2x + 1$ and $g(x) = 2x + 2$. For what values of 'x' is f(x) < g(x)?

The two graphs meet when: $x^2 + 2x + 1 = 2x + 2$

$x^2 + 2x - 2x + 1 - 2 = 0$

$x^2 - 1 = 0$

$x = \pm 1$ which are x-coordinates of the point of intersection

Substitute these x-values in f(x) or g(x) to find corresponding y-values:

$f(1) = (1)^2 + 2(1) + 1 = 4$ and $g(-1) = -2 + 2 = 0$

$\therefore$ points of intersection : $(1,4)$ and $(-1,0)$

By using the GDC it can be found that f(x) < g(x) when $-1 < x < 1$.

Practise time!

1. Using the factorization method solve for the given variable

   a. $x^2 - 5x + 6 = 0$
   b. $2x^2 - 6x - 8 = 0$
   c. $(t - 8)(t + 3) = 0$
   d. $y(y - 3) = 18$

2. Use the completing the squares method to obtain the vertex.

   a. $f(x) = 16x^2 - 28x + 6$
   b. $f(x) = 2x^2 - 9x + 4$
   c. $y = 6x^2 - 11x + 35$
   d. $y = 15x^2 - 16x + 4$

3. Find the values of m for which the quadratic $3x^2 - mx + 12$ has no real solutions

4. Find the values of u for which the quadratic $28x^2 + 60x + u$ has only one real solution

5. Sketch the graph of $f(x) = 2x^2 - 26x + 72$ without the use of a graphing calculator.

6. For the quadratic function $y = 3x^2 + 2x - 8$

   a. Find the axis of symmetry
   b. The coordinates of the vertex
   c. The x and y intercepts
   d. Sketch the function without the use of a graphing calculator

7. For what values of t will the graph of $f(x) = tx^2 - 3x - 5$ never meet the x-axis?

8. Find the range of solutions for each of the given inequalities

   a. $(x + 2)(x - 5) < 0$
   b. $(2x - 3)(x - 1) > 0$
   c. $x(x - 4) \geq 0$
   d. $(7x^2 + 22x + 3) \leq 0$

9. What is the minimum value of the function $f(x) = 18x^2 + 9x + 1$

10. For what values of n is the inequality $x^2 + nx - 24 < 0$ true for all values of x

COUNTING PRINCIPLES

1.3 Counting principles

- Permutations and combinations.
- The ability to find $\binom{n}{r}$ and ^nP_r using both the formula and technology

Not required:

1 Permutations where some objects are identical.

Concepts

- $n! = n \times (n-1)! = 1 \times 2 \times 3 \times \ldots \ldots \times (n-3) \times (n-2) \times (n-1) \times n$

- $^nP_r = \dfrac{n!}{(n-r)!}$ *(for permutations)*

- ^nC_r or $\binom{n}{r} = \dfrac{n!}{r!(n-r)!}$ *(for combinations)*

Remember!

Permutation is used when ***order*** matters. That is, the way in which a list of items are ***arranged***.

Combination is used when finding out how many ways can ***n*** number of things ***be chosen from*** a list of ***x things.***

Principles –

Multiplication Principle

Rule 1 – If any one of *n* different mutually exclusive (i.e. one outcome does not affect the other) events can occur on each of *k* trials, the number of possible outcomes is $= n^k$.

Rule 2 – if there are n_1 events on the first trial, n_2 events on the second trial, and so on until there are n_k events on the kth trial, the number of possible outcomes $= n_1 \times n_2 \times n_3 \times \ldots \ldots \times n_k$

Rule 3 – the total number of ways that n different objects can be arranged in order is $= n!$

Permutation

If there are permutations with repetitions then the number of permutation of n objects of which a items are identical, b items are identical and so on ….until k items are identical - Is given by

$$\frac{n!}{a! \times b! \times \ldots k!}$$

Combination

If the question talks about choosing a *and* b then multiply the combinations of both outcomes.

If the question asks how many combination of choosing a *or* b are possible, add both the outcomes together.

Solved examples:

Three English books, four Geography books, two mathematics books and a novel are to be placed on a student's shelf
- In how many ways can this be done if there are no restrictions?
    Since there are no restrictions, this questions is about arranging 10 (3 + 4 + 2 + 1) books on a shelf.
    This can be done in 10! ways
- In how many different ways can the books be arranged if the books of each subject remain together?

    Think of all the three English books as 1 set, all 4 Geography books as 1 set and the two mathematics book as 1 set. Plus we have 1 novel. These can be arranged in 4! ways.

    Now, the three English in the set can also be arranged within themselves. This can be done in 3! ways. Similarly, the four geography books can be arranged in 4! ways, the two mathematics books can be arranged in 2! ways , the novel can be arranged in 1! Way.

    So the total number of ways of arranging the books so that the books of a subject are together is:

    4! ×3! ×4! × 2! × 1! = 6912 ways.
- In how many of these will the novel be next to the English books?

There are 3! ways of arranging the English books, 4! ways of arranging geography books and 2! ways of arranging the math books and 3! ways of arranging the subject books (English , Geography, Mathematics) if each subject is taken as one book. And there are 2 ways of arranging the novel and the English books. So the permutations now become:

$3! \times 4! \times 2! \times 3! \times 2 = 3456$

Therefore there are 3456 ways in which the novel will be next to the English books.

There are seven boys and four girls in a school tennis team. A team of two boys and two girls will be selected to represent the school in a tennis competition.

- In how many different ways can the team be selected?

In this question, we are **choosing** 2 girls and 2 boys to play for the tennis competition. So we use combination. Out of 7 boys we choose 2, which is written as $^7C_2$ and 2 girls are to be chosen out of 4 which is written as $^4C_2$. Now the question says a team of 2 boys **and** 2 girls. This means the expressions for the combinations have to be multiplied together.

$^7C_2 \times ^4C_2 = 126$. Thus there are 126 ways of choosing the tennis team without any restrictions.

- Jake is the oldest boy in the club and Claire is the oldest girl. In how many different ways can the team be selected if it must include both of them?

In this question we have to assume that both Jake and Claire are already part of the team as the team **must** include both of them. So now there are 6 boys to be chosen from for one spot and 3 girls to be chosen from for one spot.

$^6C_1 \times ^3C_1 = 18$. There are therefore 18 ways of selecting a team with both Jake and Claire.

Practise time!

1. Twenty men and 5 women sit in a single row.

    a. In how many ways can they be arranged so that the men and women are sitting in two separate groups?

    b. 7 men and 1 woman are selected to watch a football match. In how many ways can this selection be made?

2. A team of 4 players is to be selected from a group of 11 basketball players, where 7 are boys and 4 are girls.
    a. In how many ways can this team be selected?

    b. In how many of these selections is exactly 1 boy on the team?

3. Calculate the number of ways in which 12 lollipops can be given to 5 children. If the youngest child gets 4 lollipops and the others get 2 each.

4. In how many ways can the letters of the word ASSISTANCE be arranged?

5. A, B and C are three towns. There are 8 roads connecting towns A and B and 4 roads linking B and C. how many different paths can be taken from A to C via B?

6. Find n if $^nP_5 = 15120$

7. 13 people are to shake hands at the beginning of a board meeting. How many handshakes are there?

8. How many 4-digit numbers greater than 3000 can be formed from the digits 0,1,2,3,5,7 if :

    a. None of the digits can be repeated

    b. All of the digits can be repeated

    c. The number as to be an even number

9. A multiple choice test of 27 questions contains 5 choices to choose from for each question. If a student were to guess on the test then in how many ways can the student answer all the questions on the test?

10. Write all the permutations of the letters TESSERACTS

11. Seventeen birthday cards are each labelled from 1 to 17. If 9 people are allowed to take a card each then how many ways can this be done if there are no restrictions?

12. How many different groups of 5 can be selected from 29 people?

13. Line 1 contains 5 points and Line 2 contains 7 points. In how many ways can triangles can be made from points on both the lines?

14. How many 5-digit numbers can be made using the digits 0, 1, 2, 3, 4, 7, 8 if the number formed has to be an odd number?

15. A committee of 3 is to be chosen from a group of 6 lawyers, 2 surgeons, 5 teachers and a chiropractor. Determine the number of ways such a committee can be selected if the team must have at least 1 lawyer.

MATHEMATICAL INDUCTION

1.4 Proof by mathematical induction

- Links to a wide variety of topics
- complex numbers, differentiation,
- sums of series
- Divisibility.

Introduction

- definition: the process of formulating a general result from a close examination of simplest cases

Mathematical Induction

1. Let P_n be a proposition which is defined for every integer $n \geq a$, $n \in Z$. If P_a is true, and if P_{k+1} is true whenever P_k is true, then P_n is true for all $n \geq a$.

2. i.e. if P_1 is true for a given proposition and it can be proven that P_{k+1} is true whenever P_k is true, then P_1 being true implies that P_2 is true, which implies that P_3 is true, and so on.

There are basically 3 types of questions asked on the IB and any other question is usually another version of one of these questions.

First type: Basic algebraic manipulation

Prove that: $1 + 4 + 7 + \ldots + (3n - 2) = \frac{1}{2}n(3n - 1)$

When n = 1

LHS = 1 $\qquad$ RHS = $\frac{1}{2}1(3 - 1) = 1$

So true for n = 1

Assume true for n = k

So $1 + 4 + 7 + \ldots + (3k - 2) = \frac{1}{2}k(3k - 1)$ ────── ①

Now for n = k+1

LHS: $1 + 4 + 7 + \ldots + (3k - 2) + (3(k+1)) - 2)$

Substituted by ①

$= \boxed{\frac{1}{2}k(3k-1)} + (3(k+1)) - 2)$

$= \frac{1}{2}k(3k-1) + (3k+3) - 2)$

$= \frac{k(3k-1) + 2(3k+1)}{2}$

$= \frac{3k^2 - k + 6k + 2}{2}$

$= \frac{3k^2 + 5k + 2}{2}$

$= \frac{1}{2}(k+1)(3k+2)$ ⟶ Factorization of the previous step to obtain this

Therefore if it is true for n = k it is true for n = k+1. It has been shown to be true for n = 1 so must be true for all $n (\in \mathbb{Z}^+)$. ⟶ This statement is very important. Memorize it!

Second type: Inequality

Prove that $1 + 2n < 3^n$ for all $n > 1$.

For an inequality induction rearrange the equation to bring all the terms to one side

$$= -3^n + 1 + 2n < 0$$

We can change the signs to make it

$3^n - 1 - 2n > 0$, this equation is a lot easier to work with. Unlike normal induction where you prove LHS = RHS, in the case of an inequality, you have to deduce the proof.

Now we test for n = 2 as range is given to be > 1.

$$3^2 - 1 - (2 \times 2) > 0$$

$$= 4 > 0$$

Thus expression holds true for n = 2

Assume that T (n) is true for n = k

That is, $3^k - 1 - 2k > 0$

To prove T (n) holds true for n = k + 1 , that is , to show $3^{k+1} - 1 - 2(k + 1) > 0$

LHS $= 3^{k+1} - 1 - 2(k + 1)$

$= \boxed{3 \times 3^k - 2k - 3}$ Algebraic manipulation

$= \boxed{3 \times 3^k - 6k - 3 + 4k}$

$= 3(3^k - 2k - 1) + 4k > 0$

Since $3^k - 1 - 2k > 0$ and $4k > 0$

Hence if the inequality holds true for n = k, it also holds true for n = k + 1. As it is true for n = 2, so must be true for all $n (\in \mathbb{Z}^+)$.

Third type: divisibility

Prove that $7^n + 2$ is divisible by 3

When n =1

$$\frac{7^1 + 2}{3} = 3$$

So true for n = 1

Assume true for n = k

Where, $7^k + 2 = 3m$, as $7^k + 2$ has to be a multiple of 3 to be divisible by it, it is equated to 3 multiplied by a variable m

Make 7^k the subject to give $7^k = 3m - 2$ ——— ①

To prove true for n = k + 1

$= 7^{k+1} + 2$

$= 7 \times 7^k + 2$

Substitute equation 1 above

$= 7 \times (3m - 2) + 2$

$= 21m - 14 + 2$

$= 21m - 12$

Take 3 common outside as that is the divisibility you want to prove.

$= 3(7m - 4)$

Therefore if it is true for n = k it is true for n = k+1. It has been shown to be true for n =1 so must be true for all $n \ (\in \mathbb{Z}^+)$.

Practise time!

1. $1 + 2 + 3 + \cdots .. (n-1) + n = \frac{n(n+1)}{2}$ for all $n \ \epsilon \ \mathbb{Z}^+$
2. $1^3 + 2^3 + 3^3 + \cdots .. + n^3 = \frac{n^2(n+1)^2}{4}$ for all $n \ \epsilon \ \mathbb{Z}^+$

3. $1 + 3 + 5 + \cdots + (2n - 1) = n^2$

4. $1.2 + 2.3 + 3.4 + \cdots + (n)(n+1) = \frac{n(n+1)(n+2)}{3}$

5. $\frac{1}{1.2} + \frac{1}{2.3} + \cdots + \frac{1}{(n-1)n} = \frac{(n-1)}{n}$

6. $n^2 \geq 2n + 3$ for $n \geq 3$

7. $\sum_{t=1}^{n} t(t+1) = \frac{n(n+1)(n+2)}{3}$ all $n \geq 2$

8. $\sum_{i=1}^{n}(8i - 5) = 4n^2 - n$ all $n \ \epsilon \ \mathbb{Z}^+$

9. $3 + 3^2 + 3^3 + \cdots + 3^n = \frac{3^{n+1} - 3}{2}$
10. $\sum_{i=1}^{n} \frac{1}{i(i+1)} = \frac{n}{(n+1)}$

11. $1 \times 1! + 2 \times 2! + 3 \times 3! + \cdots + n \times n! = (n+1)! - 1$

12. $1 + 5 + 13 + \cdots + (4n - 3) = \frac{n(4n-2)}{2}$

13. $3^n < n!$ for all $n \geq 7$

14. $2^n > n^2$ for all $n \geq 5$

15. $6^n - 1$ is divisible by 5 for all $n \geq 1$

16. $23^n - 1$ is divisible by 11 for all $n \geq 1$

17. $3 \mid (4^n + 8)$ for all $n \geq 0$

18. $1 + 2 + 2^2 + 2^3 + \cdots + 2^n = 2^{n+1} - 1$

19. $(1 + x)^n \geq (1 + nx)$ for all $n \geq 1$

20. $\dfrac{1}{\sqrt{1}+\sqrt{2}} + \dfrac{1}{\sqrt{2}+\sqrt{3}} + \cdots + \dfrac{1}{\sqrt{n-1}+\sqrt{n}} = \sqrt{n} - 1$

BINOMIAL EXPANSION

1.3 The binomial theorem:

- The ability to find $\binom{n}{r}$
- Expansion of $(a + b)^n$, $n \in$

Not required:

- Circular arrangements.
- Proof of binomial theorem.

Concepts

- *Binomial coefficient*

1. *defined as* ${}^nC_r = \binom{n}{r} = \dfrac{n(n-1)(n-2)\ldots(n-r+2)(n-r+1)}{r(r-1)(r-2)\ldots(2)(1)} = \dfrac{n!}{r!(n-r)!}$

2. *can be found using a graphing calculator*

3. *expansion of* $(a+b)^n \qquad a^n + \binom{n}{1}a^{n-1}b + \ldots + \binom{n}{r}a^{n-r}b^r + \ldots + b^n$

4. *To find the* $(r+1)^{th}$ *term* $\quad t_{r+1} = \binom{n}{r} \times (a)^{n-r} \times (b)^r$ where r is *one less than the term that you want to find*. For example: to find the fifth term of the expansion $r = 5 - 1 = 4$.

5. *using sigma notation:* $(a + b)^n = \displaystyle\sum_{r=0}^{n} \binom{n}{r} a^{n-r} b^r$

6. *general expansions*
$$(a+b)^2 = a^2 + 2ab + b^2$$
$$(a-b)^2 = a^2 - 2ab + b^2$$
$$(a+b)^3 = a^3 + 3a^2b + 3ab^2 + b^3$$
$$(a-b)^3 = a^3 - 3a^2b + 3ab^2 - b^3$$

Pascal's triangle

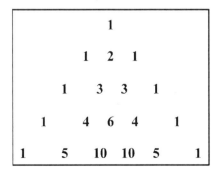

- *Number of terms in the expansion = n + 1*
- *(n+1)th row in a Pascal's triangle gives the coefficients in the expansion of $(a + b)^n$*

Additional things to remember

1. The independent term is always the term where x is raised to 0. As in, the term is 'independent' of x.

2. If asked to find the coefficient of x^n (for example x^2) in the multiplication of two binomial expansions,
(Such as, $(x + 1)^3 \times (2x + 3)^2$), expand both binomial expressions and multiply coefficients of terms whose x multiplies to give a 2nd degree x term.

Solved examples:

- Expand and simplify $(x^2 + \frac{5}{x})^3$.

$$^3C_0 \times (x^2)^3 + {}^3C_1 \times (x^2)^2 \times (\frac{5}{x}) + {}^3C_2 \times (x^2) \times (\frac{5}{x})^2 + {}^3C_3 \times (\frac{5}{x})^3$$

$$= (x^6) + 15x^3 + 75 + \frac{125}{x^3}$$

- Determine the term independent of x in the expansion of $(1 + 3x)^5(2 - x)^2$.

This means that we have to find the coefficient of the term with x^0.

Expansion of $(2 - x)^2 = 4 - 4x + x^2$

$(4 - 4x + x^2)(1 + 3x)^5$

Since there are no negative powers of x in the expansion of $(1 + 3x)^5$. The term independent of x can only be obtained by multiplying the coefficients of terms of x^0. So the term independent of x in the expansion of $(2 - x)^2$ is 4 and in the case of $(1 + 3x)^5$ it is just 1.

So 4×1 =4.

These are the two types of questions that can come on the exam, either normal binomial expansion or expansion of two binomial terms and their multiplication to obtain the coefficient of x^n.

Practice time!

1. Expand $(x^2 - \frac{2}{x})^4$

2. Find n and a if the first three terms in the expansion of $(1 + ax)^n$ are
   $1 + 2x + \frac{5}{3}x^2$

3. If $(2 + ax)^4$ expands to $16 + 64x + \cdots$ then what is the value of a?

4. Find the 3rd term in the expansion of $(1 + x^2)^8$

5. Find the 4th term in the expansion of $(1 + 2x)^6$

6. Find the 5th term in the expansion of $(x + \frac{1}{x})^8$

7. Find the 6th term in the expansion of $(x - \frac{1}{x^2})^{10}$

8. Find the term containing x^{10} in the expansion of $(5 + 2x^2)^7$

9. Find the middle term in the expansion of $(x^2 + \frac{2}{x})^8$

10. Find the middle term in the expansion of $(x + \frac{2}{x})^{20}$

11. Find the coefficient of x^9 in $(2 - x^3)^{10}$

12. Find the coefficient of x^5 in $(3x - 2)^8$

13. Find the term independent of x in the expansion of $(x + \frac{2}{x})^4$

14. Find the constant term in the expansion of $(x - \frac{2}{x^2})^9$

15. Find the term independent of x in the expansion of $(2x + \frac{1}{x^2})^{11}$

16. Find the constant term in the expansion of $(3x^2 - \frac{2}{x})^9$

17. Find the term independent of x in the expansion of $(x - \frac{1}{x^2})^{18}$

18. Two consecutive terms in the expansion of $(2x + 3)^9$ have the same coefficient. What terms are those and what is the equal coefficient?

19. Find the value of n and k if kxy^6 is the term independent of x in the expansion of $(2x + 3y^2)^n$

20. Prove that the constant term in the expansion of $(x^4 - \frac{2}{x})^n$ is non zero only when n is a multple of 5.

POLYNOMIALS

2.5 Polynomial functions and their graphs.
   The factor and remainder theorems.
   The fundamental theorem of algebra.
   The graphical significance of repeated factors.
   The relationship between the degree of polynomial function and the possible numbers of x-intercepts.

   - $P(x) = a_n x^n + a_{n-1} x^{n-1} + \cdots + a_2 x^2 + a_1 x + a_0, \ a_n \neq 0$

1. a_n is the leading coefficient
2. a_0 is the constant term
3. a_r is the coefficient of x^r for $r = 0,1,2,\ldots,n$
4. n is the degree of the polynomal (highest power of the variable)

Operations of polynomials:

Addition and subtraction – to add or subtract two polynomials together, collect terms with the same power for x and then add or subtract the terms.

For e.g. Add $P(x) = x^3 + 2x^2 + 1$ and $Q(x) = 2x^3 + 4x + 2$

$(x^3 + 2x^3) + (2x^2) + (4x) + (1 + 2) = 3x^3 + 2x^2 + 4x + 3$

The same applies for subtraction.

Multiplication with a constant k – If $P(x)$ is a polynomial and you have to find out what $kP(x)$ is then every term in the polynomial is multiplied by the constant k.

For e.g. If $P(x)$ is $= 2x^3 - x^2 + 1$, find $aP(x)$, where a is a constant term

$= 2ax^3 - ax^2 + a$

Multiplication of polynomials - Multiply each term of polynomial 1 by each term of polynomial 2, then collect the terms with the same power.

For e.g. Find the product of $(2x^2 - 3x + 5)(3x - 1)$

$= (2x^2 \times 3x) + (2x^2 \times -1) + (-3x \times 3x) + (-3x \times -1) + (5 \times 3x) + (5 \times -1)$

$= 6x^3 - 2x^2 - 9x^2 + 3x + 15x - 5$

$= 6x^3 - 11x^2 + 18x - 5$

Division of polynomials- In this case, synthetic division is used

For e.g. $\dfrac{x^2 + 2x - 3}{x + 2}$

	1	2	-3
-2		-2	0
	1	0	-3

So the answer becomes $x - \frac{3}{x+2}$

The remainder theorem

This is when you only want to find the remainder of a division operation between two polynomials

If $\frac{x^2+2x-3}{(x+a)}$ then to find the remainder you first equate $x + a = 0$, so $x = -a$. Now substitute this value for x in the dividend which is the polynomial $x^2 + 2x - 3$. So the remainder of the polynomial becomes $(-a)^2 + 2(-a) - 3 = a^2 - 2a - 3$. And **remember** if the remainder in such divisions is 0 then it means that the divisor is a root of the dividend.

Solved example:

- Find the value of k in the polynomial $x^3 - kx^2 - x + 2$ if the remainder when divided by $x + 2$ is 20.

So we know that $\frac{x^3-kx^2-x+2}{x+2}$ gives a remainder of 20.

$x + 2 = 0$, so $x = -2$

$(-2)^3 - k(-2)^2 - (-2) + 2 = 20$

$-8 - 4k + 4 = 20$

$-4k - 4 = 20$

$-4k = 24$

$k = -6$

The factor theorem

As the name suggests, this method is used to find the factors of a polynomial. That is, values of x for which the polynomial = 0.

$(x - a)$ is a factor of $P(x)$ only if $P(a) = 0$

Solved example:

$4x^3 - cx^2 + dx - 6$ Is completely divisible by $(x - 3)$ and $(x + 2)$. Find c and d.

When the question says completely divisible then it means for that x value the polynomial = 0

So here,

$x - 3 = 0 \ so \ x = 3$

And $4(3)^3 - c(3)^2 + d(3) - 6 = 0$

$108 - 9c + 3d - 6 = 0$

$102 - 9c + 3d = 0$

$9c - 3d = 102$ ──────── ①

$x + 2 = 0 \ so \ x = -2$

$4(-2)^3 - c(-2)^2 + d(-2) - 6 = 0$

$-32 - 4c - 2d - 6 = 0$

$-38 - 4c - 2d = 0$

$4c + 2d = -38$ ──────── ②

$9c - 3d = 102$

Simplifying the simultaneous equations give

$2c + d = -19$

$3c - d = 34$

$5c = 15$

$c = 3$

$2c + d = -19$

$2(3) + d = -19$

When a graph of a polynomial is plotted and it touches the x axis, the points where it touches are the roots of the polynomial. For the polynomial $(x+3)^2 - 2$ the graph is plotted below

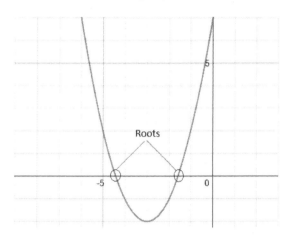

Polynomial Equations

The expression $P(x) = 0$ where $P(x)$ is of the form $a_n x^n + a_{n-1} x^{n-1} + \cdots + a_2 x^2 + a_1 x + a_0$ is known as a polynomial **equation.**

Solved example:

solve $x^3 - 6x^2 + 11x - 6 = 0$

If this question comes in paper 1, you would have to solve for the first factor by trial and error.

So here let's try $(x - 1)$.

$P(1) = 1 - 6 + 11 - 6 = 0$ Here the first trial worked. Now we know that $(x - 1)$ is a factor. The other two factors can be found through synthetic division

	1	-6	11	-6
1		1	-5	6
	1	-5	6	0

so the quadratic obtained is $x^2 - 5x + 6$ the remainder need not be written as it is zero. Now factorize this polynomial as you would factorize any other quadratic

$x^2 - 3x - 2x + 6$

$x(x - 3) - 2(x - 3)$

$(x - 2)(x - 3)$

So the factors of the cubic polynomial at the start is $(x - 1)(x - 2)(x - 3)$

Polynomial Inequations

These are polynomial equations of the form $P(x) > 0, P(x) \geq 0, P(x) < 0 \text{ and } P(x) \leq 0$.

Solved example:

- Find $x^3 + 3x^2 - 6x - 8 > 0$

Let $P(x) = x^3 + 3x^2 - 6x - 8$
Using the graphing calculator we get

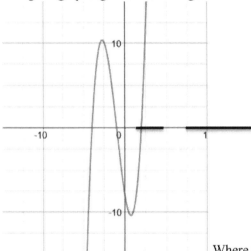

Where the roots are $-1, -4 \text{ and } 2$

So the factors are $(x + 1)(x + 4)(x - 2)$
We can write the polynomial inequality as $(x + 1)(x + 4)(x - 2) > 0$
To get $-4 < x < -1$ and $x > 2$ as depicted by the bold black lines.

Sketching of polynomials

If the polynomial has distinct roots then the line of the polynomial just cuts the x-axis at these places as shown below.

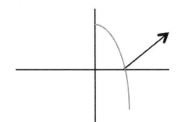

Distinct root. For e.g. if a polynomial has roots $(x - a)(x - b)(x - c)$ where $a \neq b \neq c$. Then the roots just cut the x-axis

Significance of repeated roots

For a polynomial such as $x^2 - 4x + 4$ the factors are $(x - 2)(x - 2)$ this is repeated roots. When a polynomial has roots of the form $(x - a)^2$, then the curve will not cut through, but rather just touch the x-axis.

Cubic polynomials

- continuous smooth curves

- cuts the x-axis at least once = at least one real zero

- for P(x) = a(x-α)(x-β)(x-ɣ) where α, β, ɣ ∈ R, the graph will cross the x-axis at these points (x-intercepts)

- for P(x) = a(x-α)²(x-β) where α, β ∈ R, the graph will touch the x-axis at (α, 0) and cross the x-axis at (β, 0)

- for P(x) = a(x-α)³, x∈ R, the x-axis is a tangent to the graph at (α, 0)

- for P(x) = (x-α)(ax² + bx + c), Δ< 0, the graph cuts the x-axis only at (α, 0) and the other 2 zeros are complex and do not appear on the graph

Quartic polynomials

1. let 'a' be the coefficient of x^4
   - if $a > 0$ the graph opens upwards
   - if $a < 0$ the graph opens downwards

2. if $a > 0$ and the polynomial is fully factorized
   - for a single factor (x-α) the graph cuts x-axis at α
   - for a square factor (x-α)² the graph touches x-axis at α
   - or a cubed factor (x-α)³ the graph cuts the x-axis at α and is a tangent to it at that point
     • for a quadruple factor (x-α)⁴ the graph touches the x-axis at α and is a tangent to it at that point

- if a>0, and the polynomial has 1 real quadratic factor with Δ< 0, two roots would be complex and two would be real (x intercepts)
1. if a>0 has 2 real quadratic factors with Δ< 0, all roots are complex so the graph will have no x-intercepts.

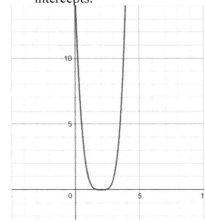

$(x - \alpha)^4$

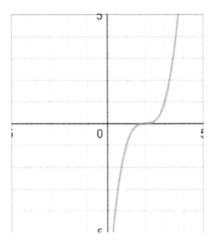

$(x - \alpha)^3$

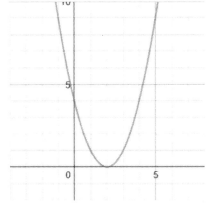

$(x - \alpha)^2$

Note – there are as many roots as the highest degree of the polynomial. If the polynomial is a degree three polynomial then there are three roots. All three may be real or one root may be real and the other two imaginary. The imaginary roots always come in pairs. This is explored in greater detail in complex numbers.

Practice time!

1. Find the remainder when $x^3 + x^2 - 16x - 16$ is divided by $(x + 1)$
2. Write down the polynomial with zeroes -5, 4 and 1
3. Solve the equation $x^3 - 5x^2 + 8x - 4 = 0$
4. $(x - 7)$ is a factor of the polynomial $P(x) = ux^3 - 16x^2 - kx + m$. Solve to find u, k and m. Given that $P(x)$ passes the x axis at $x = -1$ and $x = \frac{2}{3}$. And hence fully factorize $P(x)$.
5. The remainder when $P(x)$ is divided by $(x - 1)$ is 9 and when it is divided by $(x + 2)$ the remainder is 0. Find the value of a and b if $P(x) = x^3 - ax^2 + b + 16$.
6. Find the remainder when $x^3 + x^2 + x - 3$ is divided by $(x - 8)$.
7. Sketch the graph of the polynomial $x^3 - 5x^2 - 2x + 24$.
8. Show that the cubic polynomial $x^3 + 8x^2 + 22x + 20$ has no other real roots apart from $(x + 2)$.
9. solve the following inequalities:
    a. $(x - 1)^2(x + 3) \geq 0$
    b. $(x + 2)(x - 3)(x + 1) < 0$
    c. $(x - 5)(x + 4)(x + 7) \leq 0$
10. Sketch the graph of the polynomial $P(x) = (x - 5)(x^2 - 10x + 25)$

COMPLEX NUMBERS

1.5 Complex numbers: the number $i = \sqrt{-1}$;
The terms real part, imaginary part, conjugate, modulus and argument.
Cartesian form $z = a + ib$.
Sums, products and quotients of complex numbers

1.6 Modulus–argument (polar) form
$z = r(\cos\theta + i\sin\theta) = r\,\text{cis}\,\theta = re^{i\theta}$

1.7 Powers of complex numbers: de Moivre's theorem. n^{th} roots of a complex number.

1.8 Conjugate roots of polynomial equations with real coefficients.

Complex numbers are those numbers which are a combination of a real number and an imaginary number. It is common in quadratic equations when the discriminant $b^2 - 4ac < 0$ there are no real solutions. We usually ignore these answers when solving problems in math class. But in this chapter we will be dealing with the imaginary roots

Representations of complex numbers

- Cartesian form: $z = a + bi$, where $a = \text{Re}(z)$ which is the real part, $b = \text{Im}(z)$ is the imaginary part and $a, b \in \mathbb{R}$
- complex plane: complex numbers can be plotted on a complex (or Argand) plane because the Cartesian form shows that there is a 1→1 relationship between $a + bi$ and the point (a, b)
- Argand diagram: the representation of complex numbers using vectors on an Argand plane
- polar form: using modulus and argument of z

Properties of argument functions

1. $\arg(z_1 z_2) = \arg(z_1) + \arg(z_2) = \theta_1 + \theta_2$
2. $\arg(z_1 z_2 \ldots z_n) = \arg(z_1) + \arg(z_2) + \cdots + \arg(z_n) = \theta_1 + \theta_2 + \ldots + \theta_n$
3. $\arg(z_1^n) = n \times \arg(z_1)$
4. $\arg\left(\frac{1}{z_2}\right) = -\arg(z_2)$
5. $\arg\left(\frac{z_1}{z_2}\right) = \arg(z_1) - \arg(z_2)$
    1. $\arg(z_1^*) = -\arg(z_1) = -\theta_1$

Argand diagrams
- e.g. $\overline{OP} = \begin{pmatrix} x \\ y \end{pmatrix}$ represents $x + iy$
- all real numbers with $y = 0$ lie on the real axis
- all purely imaginary numbers with $x = 0$ lie on the imaginary axis
- the origin lies on both axes and corresponds to $z = 0$ (real number)
- complex numbers for which $x, y \neq 0$ lie in one of the four quadrants
- conjugates are reflections of each other in the real axis
- e.g. if $\overline{OP} = \begin{pmatrix} x \\ y \end{pmatrix}$ represents $z = x + iy$ then $\overline{OP'} = \begin{pmatrix} x \\ -y \end{pmatrix}$ represents its conjugate $z^* = x - iy$

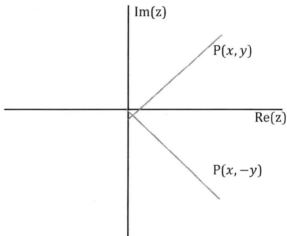

Now let us try to solve some basic problems that you may come across :

1. given that $\dfrac{z}{z+1} = 1 + 2i$, find z in the form of $x + yi$

Do NOT substitute $z = x + yi$ in the beginning. The first step is to simplify

$z = (z + 1) \times (1 + 2i)$

$z = z + 2zi + 1 + 2i$

$0 = (2z + 2)i + 1$

Now we can substitute the $x + yi$ in place of z.

$0 = (2(x + yi) + 2)i + 1$

$0 = (2x + 2yi + 2)i + 1$

$0 = 2xi + (2yi \times i) + 2i + 1$

$0 = 2xi - 2y + 2i + 1$

Both the real part and imaginary part of the equation above is zero.

$2x + 2 = 0$

$1 - 2y = 0$

so then $y = \frac{1}{2}$ and $x = -1$

So $z = -1 + \frac{1}{2}i$

modulus:

magnitude of a complex number $z = a + bi$

i.e. length of the vector $\binom{a}{b}$ which is also the distance of (a, b) from the origin

formula: $|z| = \sqrt{a^2 + b^2}$

- distance in the number plane

1   if $z_1 \equiv \overrightarrow{OP_1}$ and $z_2 \equiv \overrightarrow{OP_2}$ then $|z_1 - z_2|$ is the distance between P_1 and P_2

Properties of modulus:

2   $|z^*| = |z|$

3   $|z|^2 = zz^*$

4   $|z_1 z_2| = |z_1||z_2|$

5   $\left|\frac{z_1}{z_2}\right| = \frac{|z_1|}{|z_2|}$ if $z_2 \neq 0$

6   $|z_1 z_2 z_3 \ldots z_n| = |z_1||z_2||z_3|\ldots|z_n|$ for $n \in Z+$

7   $|z^n| = |z|^n$ for $n \in Z^+$

Argument and polar form

> Proof of distance formula: *let P_1 and P_2 be two points in the complex plane corresponding to complex numbers z_1 and z_2*
>
> $|z_1 - z_2| = |(x_1 + y_1 i) - (x_2 + y_2 i)|$
>
> $= |(x_1 - x_2) + (y_1 - y_2)i|$
>
> $= \sqrt{(x_1 - x_2)^2 + (y_1 - y_2)^2}$
>
> $\overrightarrow{P_2 P_1} = \overrightarrow{P_2 O} + \overrightarrow{OP_1}$

$$= -z_2 + z_1$$

$$= z_1 - z_2$$

$$\therefore |z_1 - z_2| = |\overrightarrow{P_2P_1}| \text{ (distance between } P_1 \text{ and } P_2\text{)}$$

If $\overrightarrow{OP}$ represents the complex number $z = a + bi$, then the angle Θ between $\overrightarrow{OP}$ and the positive real axis is called the argument of z (arg z). It describes the direction of a complex number.

Note: **real** numbers have an argument $= 0$ or π while purely **imaginary** numbers have an argument $= \frac{\pi}{2}$ or $\frac{-\pi}{2}$.

Derivation of polar form: a point P lying on a circle with center (0, 0) and radius 'r' has coordinates (rcosθ, rsinθ)

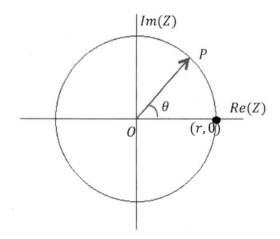

$\therefore$ on an Argand plane, $\overrightarrow{OP}$ represents the complex number $z = r\cos\theta + i\,r\sin\theta$

The polar form, $z = r\cos\theta + i\,r\sin\theta = r(\cos\theta + i\sin\theta) = rcis\theta$ is a different way to represent complex numbers using modulus and argument. It uses – multiplication, division, and finding powers and roots of complex numbers.

1. $\theta = arg\ z$ and $r = |z|$ ∴ $z = |z|\ cis\theta$
2. if $z = |z|cis\theta$ then $z* = |z|\ cis(-\theta)$
3. multiplication: if a complex number 'z' is multiplied by $rcis\theta$, its modulus is multiplied by r and its argument is increased by θ.

Properties of $z = rcis\theta = \boldsymbol{a + bi}$:

- $r = |z| = \sqrt{a^2 + b^2}$
- $tan\theta = \frac{b}{a}$
- $cos\theta = \frac{a}{\sqrt{a^2+b^2}}$
- $sin\theta = \frac{b}{\sqrt{a^2+b^2}}$
- $cis\theta \times cis\varphi = cis(\theta + \varphi)$
- $\frac{cis\theta}{cis\varphi} = cis(\theta - \varphi)$
- $cis(\theta + k2\pi) = cis\theta$ for all $k \in Z$
- $zw = |z||w|\ cis(\theta + \varphi)$
- $\frac{z}{w} = \frac{|z|}{|w|}\ cis(\theta - \varphi)$

Euler's form

- Euler proved that $e^{i\theta} = cos\theta + isin\theta$ (using calculus)
- ∴ the complex number $z = |z|cis\theta$ can also be written as $z = |z|\ e^{i\theta}$

De Moivre's theorem

- This theorem states that $(|z|\times cis\theta)^n = |z|^n cis(n\theta)$ for all rational 'n'. It allows easy calculation of powers of complex numbers
- Although you do not need to know this, the proof using mathematical induction is :

$P\_n: (|z|cis\theta)^n = |z|^n cis(n\theta)\ for\ n \in Z^+$

$if\ n = 1,$

$(|z|cis\theta)^1 = |z|cis(\theta)$ ∴ P_1 is true

$if\ P_k\ is\ true, then: (|z|cis\theta)^k = |z|^k\ cis(k\theta)$

∴ $(|z|cis\theta)^{k+1} = (|z|cis\theta)^k \times |z|cis(\theta)$

$$= |z|^k \, cis(k\theta) \times |z| cis(\theta)$$

$$= |z|^{k+1} \, cis(k\theta + \theta)$$

$$= |z|^{k+1} \, cis(k+1)\theta$$

P_1 is true, P_{k+1} is true when P_k is true

$\therefore P_n$ is true for all $n \in Z^+$

Roots of complex numbers

We use De Moivre's theorem to find roots of complex numbers for example: let $z^n = c$, $n \in Z^+$ and 'c' is a complex number .the nth roots of complex number 'c' are the 'n' solutions of $z^n = c$. There are exactly 'n' nth roots of 'c'. If $c \in R$, the complex roots occur in conjugate pairs. If $c \notin R$, the complex roots do not all occur in conjugate pairs

- the roots of z^n all have the same modulus $= |c|^{\frac{1}{n}}$
- On an argand diagram: the roots are equally spaced on a circle with radius $= |c|^{\frac{1}{n}}$

1 methods to find roots: factorization, nth root method (preferable)

Most questions seen in the exam would have to do with the concept of De Moivre's theorem such as this one below.

Let $\omega = \cos\left(\frac{3\pi}{4}\right) + i \sin\left(\frac{3\pi}{4}\right)$

- Find what the value of ω^4 is.
  The way to tackle this problem is by converting the form given above into cis form.
  $$\omega = cis\left(\frac{3\pi}{4}\right)$$
  Now $\omega^4 = \left(cis\left(\frac{3\pi}{4}\right)\right)^4$
  According to De Moivre's Theorem, the power comes down and is multiplied by what is inside the bracket
  $$\omega^4 = \left(cis\left(4 \times \frac{3\pi}{4}\right)\right)$$
  $$\omega^4 = cis(3\pi)$$
  This expands out to be
  $$\omega^4 = \cos(3\pi) + i\sin(3\pi)$$
  so $\omega^4 = -1$

Conjugate root theorem:

Another important theorem that you will have to apply in the exam is the conjugate root theorem. This theorem states that the complex roots of a polynomial with real coefficients occur in pairs.

For example :

The polynomial $5x^2 + 2x + 1$ has a root $\frac{-1}{5} + \frac{2}{5}i$. then according to the conjugate root theorem, the other root will be this root's conjugate which is $\frac{-1}{5} - \frac{2}{5}i$.

Practice time!

1. Given that $z = 2 + 3i$ and $\omega = 1 + 2i$, find the following

    a) z^* b) $z\omega$ c) $\omega\omega^*$

2. Express the complex number $\frac{1+3i}{2-5i}$ in the form $a + bi$.

3. Find the modulus of the following complex numbers.

    a) $5 + 4i$ b) $7 - 3i$

4. Show the following complex numbers on an argand diagram

    a) $9 + 2i$ b) $6i$ c) $4 - 3i$

5. What is the modulus and argument of $1 + \sqrt{2}i$? Express this in the polar form.

6. Let $z_1 = 4cis\left(\frac{7\pi}{3}\right)$ and $z_2 = 5cis\left(\frac{4\pi}{9}\right)$. Determine the value of $\arg(z_1 z_2)$.

7. Express $(2 + \sqrt{3}i)^4$ in the form $a + bi$.

8. What is $z^n + \frac{1}{z^n}$ when $z = cis\frac{2\pi}{5}$

9. Solve the equation $x^2 + 3x + 5 = 0$. Solutions may be complex.

10. Factorize $x^3 + 2x^2 + x + 2$.

CIRCULAR FUNCTIONS AND TRIGONOMETRY

3.1 The circle: radian measure of angles.

Length of an arc; area of a sector.

3.2 Definition of $\cos\theta$, $\sin\theta$ and $\tan\theta$ in terms of the unit circle.

Exact values of sin, cos and tan of $0, \frac{\pi}{6}, \frac{\pi}{4}, \frac{\pi}{3}, \frac{\pi}{2}$ and their multiples.

Definition of the reciprocal trigonometric ratios , $\csc\theta$ and $\cot\theta$.

Pythagorean identities: $\cos^2\theta + \sin^2\theta = 1$

$1 + \tan^2\theta = \sec^2\theta\,; 1 + \cot^2\theta = \csc^2\theta$

3.3 Compound angle identities.

Double angle identities.

Not required:

Proof of compound angle identities

3.4 Composite functions of the form $f(x) = a\sin(b(x+c)) + d$.

3.5 The inverse functions $x \rightarrow \arcsin x$, $x \rightarrow \arccos x$, $x \rightarrow \arctan x$; their domains and ranges;

Their graphs.

3.6 Algebraic and graphical methods of solving trigonometric equations in a finite interval,

Including the use of trigonometric identities and factorization.

Not required:

The general solution of trigonometric equations

3.7 The cosine rule

The sine rule including the ambiguous case.

Area of a triangle as $\frac{1}{2} \times ab \times sinC$

Degree measure

- $360°$ is one revolution $\therefore 1° = \frac{1}{360}$th of one revolution
- further, 1 minute $(1') = \frac{1}{60}$th of $1°$ and 1 second $(1'') = \frac{1}{60}$th of $1'$

Degrees $\rightarrow \times \frac{\pi}{180} \rightarrow$ radians

Radian measure

- definition: an angle has a measure of 1 radian (1^c) if it is
- subtended at the center of a circle by an arc of the length equal to the radius of the circle.
- 'c' is used to represent radian measure, but usually is omitted
- if the radius of the circle is 'r', then the arc length is Given by $r\theta$ where θ is the angle subtended by the radii of the circle.
- half of the circumference of a circle will subtend an a
- angle of π radians
- π radians $= 180°$. This idea must be used when converting
- angles from one form to the other.

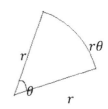

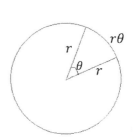

Arc Length and Sector Area

- arc length (l)
  - for angle in radians, $l = r\theta$
  - for angle in degrees, $l = \frac{\theta}{360} \times 2\pi r$
- sector area (A)
  - for angle in radians, $A = \frac{1}{2}r^2\theta$
  - for angle in degrees, $A = \frac{\theta}{360} \times \pi r^2$

The Unit Circle

- if P(x,y) is any point on a circle with center (0,0) and radius 'r',

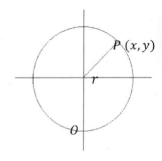

$$OP = r$$

$$\sqrt{(x-0)^2 + (y-0)^2} = r$$

$\therefore x^2 + y^2 = r^2 \rightarrow$ eqn of circle with center (0,0) and radius r

- unit circle: a circle with center (0,0) and radius 1, with equation $x^2 + y^2 = 1$
- angle (θ) measurement: θ is positive for anticlockwise rotations and negative for clockwise rotations

Trigonometric ratios

- for a point P on the unit circle, cosθ is the x-coordinate and sinθ is the y-coordinate
  - from the unit circle equation $x^2 + y^2 = 1$, **$\cos^2\theta + \sin^2\theta = 1$**
  - for all points on the unit circle $-1 \leq x \leq 1$ and $-1 \leq y \leq 1$, so **$-1 \leq \cos\theta \leq 1$ and $-1 \leq \sin\theta \leq 1$**
- the position of the point Q relative to A is defined as the tangent function
- trigonometric ratios are periodic: there are 2π radians in 1 revolution, so if an integer multiple of 2π is added to θ^c, then the position of a point P on the unit circle remains unchanged
- i.e. for θ in radians and k ∈ Z
  - $\cos(\theta + 2k\pi) = \cos\theta$
  - $\sin(\theta + 2k\pi) = \sin\theta$

Let P(a,b) be a point lying on the unit circle in the 1st quadrant. OP makes an angle θ with the x-axis.

$$\cos\theta = \frac{a}{1} = a$$

$$\sin\theta = \frac{b}{1} = b$$

- $\tan(\theta + k\pi) = \tan\theta$ (because $\tan(\theta + \pi) = \frac{-b}{-a} = \frac{b}{a}$)
- This diagram can be used to find out the angles. To determine wether the angles will be negative depending on the quadrant.

Sine is positive	All are positive
Tan is positive	Cos is positive

Here is a pneumonic to help you remember:

All Students Take Coffee

θ degrees	0	30	45	60	90
θ radians	0	$\frac{\pi}{6}$	$\frac{\pi}{4}$	$\frac{\pi}{3}$	$\frac{\pi}{2}$
Sine	0	$\frac{1}{2}$	$\frac{1}{\sqrt{2}}$	$\frac{\sqrt{3}}{2}$	1
Cosine	1	$\frac{\sqrt{3}}{2}$	$\frac{1}{\sqrt{2}}$	$\frac{1}{2}$	0
Tangent	0	$\frac{1}{\sqrt{3}}$	1	$\sqrt{3}$	∞

Applications of the unit circle

To find trigonometric ratios using the identity $\cos^2\theta + \sin^2\theta = 1$

Solved example:

Find the possible values of $\cos\theta$ for

$$\sin\theta = \frac{2}{3}$$

$$\cos^2\theta + \left(\frac{2}{3}\right)^2 = 1$$

$$\cos^2\theta = \frac{5}{9}$$

$$\cos\theta = \pm\frac{\sqrt{5}}{3}$$

To find angles which have a particular sine, cosine, or tangent

Solved example:

Find the two angles θ on the unit circle, with $0 \leq \theta \leq 2\pi$, such that $\cos\theta = -\frac{2}{3}$.

using the calculator, $\cos^{-1}\left(-\frac{2}{3}\right) \approx 2.30$

since $0 \leq \theta \leq 2\pi$,

$\theta \approx \mathbf{2.30}$ or $2\pi - 2.30 = \mathbf{3.98}$

Negative and complementary angles

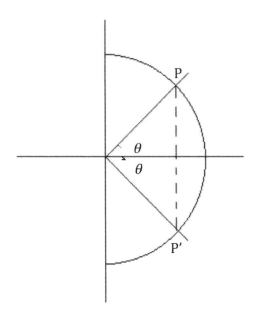

The negative of angle θ is −θ

P' $(\cos(-\theta), \sin(-\theta))$ is a reflection of P $(\cos\theta, \sin\theta)$ in the x-axis

∴ They have the same x-coordinate but the y-coordinate of P' is reflected, so it is negative.

$\cos(-\theta) = \cos\theta$

$\sin(-\theta) = -\sin\theta$

$\tan(-\theta) = \dfrac{-\sin\theta}{\cos\theta} = -\tan\theta$

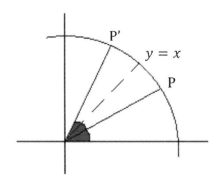

The complement of angle θ is $\frac{\pi}{2} - \theta$

The shaded angle formed by P' $= \frac{\pi}{2} - \theta$

∴ P' has coordinates $\left(\cos\left(\frac{\pi}{2} - \theta\right), \sin\left(\frac{\pi}{2} - \theta\right)\right)$

Also, P' is the reflection of P in y = x. So the coordinates of P' are $(\sin\theta, \cos\theta)$

$$\cos\left(\frac{\pi}{2} - \theta\right) = \sin\theta$$

$$\sin\left(\frac{\pi}{2} - \theta\right) = \cos\theta$$

Example: Find the exact value of $\sin\frac{4\pi}{3}$

Using $\sin\frac{\pi}{3} = \frac{\sqrt{3}}{2}$, $\sin\frac{4\pi}{3} = -\frac{\sqrt{3}}{2}$,

Non-right angled triangle Trigonometry

Introduction

- to calculate area of triangle, we can use base and height in the formula
- $A = \frac{1}{2} \times \text{base} \times h$
- in cases when 'h' is unknown, trigonometry can be used to calculate the area
- case 1: using all three sides
    - Heron's formula: $A = \sqrt{s(s-a)(s-b)(s-c)}$ where $s = \frac{a+b+c}{2}$
    - can be proven using cosine rule
- case 2: using two sides and included angle (e.g. 'c', 'a', and angle B)
    - acute triangles
    $h = AD$
    $\sin C = \frac{h}{b}$, so $h = b\sin C$

    - obtuse triangles
    $\sin(180° - C) = \frac{h}{b}$
    so $h = b\sin(180° - C) = b\sin C$
    - $\therefore$ Area $(A) = \frac{1}{2} \times \text{base} \times h = \frac{1}{2} \times \mathbf{ab \times \sin C}$
    - i.e. the area of a triangle is half the product of two sides and the sine of the included angle

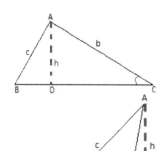

The cosine rule:

Involves the sides and angles of a triangle

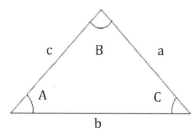

$a^2 = b^2 + c^2 - 2bc \cos A$

$b^2 = a^2 + c^2 - 2ac \cos B$

$c^2 = a^2 + b^2 - 2ab \cos A$

The sine rule:

$\frac{a}{\sin A} = \frac{b}{\sin B} = \frac{c}{\sin C}$ or $\frac{\sin A}{a} = \frac{\sin B}{b} = \frac{\sin C}{c}$

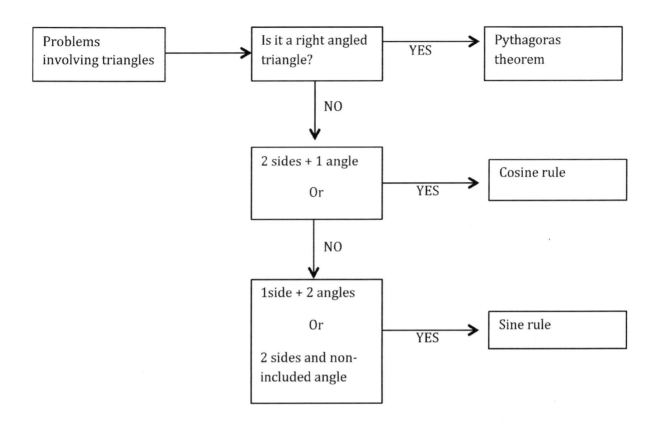

Trigonometric Functions

Introduction

- trigonometric functions can be used to model periodic phenomena
- examples of periodic phenomena: monthly temperatures, phases of the moon
- periodic function: a function which repeats in a horizontal direction,
- in intervals of the same length

1 period (of a periodic function):
    the length of one repetition or cycle

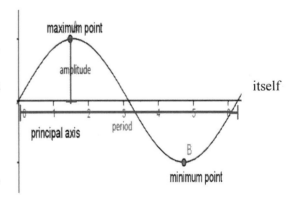

2 e.g. f(x) is a periodic function with a period 'p'
   $\Leftrightarrow$ f(x+p) = f(x) for all 'x', and 'p' is the smallest positive value for this to be true
   - periodic phenomena often show **wave** patterns

3 principal axis: a horizontal line with the equation $y = \frac{max+min}{2}$ about which a wave oscillates

4 maximum point: occurs at the top of a crest
   • minimum point: occurs at the bottom of a trough

- amplitude: distance between a maximum/minimum and the principal axis, $A = \frac{max - min}{2}$

Sine function:

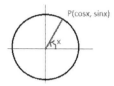

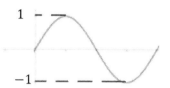

The values of $\sin x$ from the unit circle are projected onto the x- and y- axes to get a graph $y = \sin x$. 'x' is usually in radians, unless otherwise indicated

Equation: $y = \sin x$

Period: 2π

Maximum: 1, Minimum: -1

Amplitude: 1

Range: $-1 \leq y \leq 1$

The general form of the equation $y = \sin x \rightarrow y = a\sin(b(x - c)) + d$

$y = a\sin x \quad a \neq 0$

1. vertical stretch of y = cos x with scale factor |a|
2. amplitude = |a|
3. if a < 0, graph is also reflected in x-axis

$y = \sin bx \quad b > 0$

- horizontal stretch of y = cos x with scale factor $\frac{1}{b}$
- period = $\frac{2\pi}{b}$

$y = \sin(x - c) + d$

- translation of y = cos x through vector $\begin{pmatrix} c \\ d \end{pmatrix}$

Solved example:

How is $y = \sin x$ transformed into $y = 2\sin\left(3\left(x - \frac{\pi}{4}\right)\right) + 1$? Sketch the graphs.

Step 1: double the amplitude of y = sin x to get y = 2sin x

Step 2: divide period by 3 to get $y = 2\sin 3x$

Step 3: translate by $\begin{pmatrix} \frac{\pi}{4} \\ 1 \end{pmatrix}$ to get y = $2\sin(3(x - \frac{\pi}{4})) + 1$

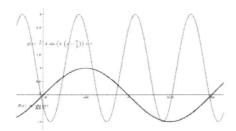

Cosine Function:

If the movement of angle 'x' is viewed from the perspective of point P, the values of cos x can be projected onto a graph to get $y = \cos x$.

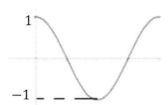

equation: $y = \cos x$

Period: 2π

Amplitude: 1

Range: $-1 \leq y \leq 1$

Sine vs. cosine function

- identical shape
- cosine function is $\frac{\pi}{2}$ units left of the sine function (horizontal translation
- i.e. $\cos x = \sin(x + \frac{\pi}{2})$
-

The general form of the equation $y = \cos x \to y = a\cos(b(x - c)) + d$

$y = a\cos x \quad a \neq 0$

1. vertical stretch of y = sin x with scale factor |a|
2. amplitude = |a|
3. if a < 0, graph is also reflected in x-axis

$y = \cos bx \quad b > 0$

- horizontal stretch of y = sin x with scale factor $\frac{1}{b}$
- period = $\frac{2\pi}{b}$

$y = \cos(x - c) + d$

- translation of y = sin x through vector $\binom{c}{d}$

Sketch the graph of $y = \cos(2x)$.

Step 1: divide the period of $y = \cos x$ by 2 to get $y = \cos 2x$

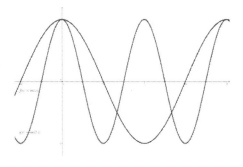

Tangent function

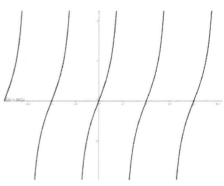

- from the unit circle, the definition of the tangent function is: $\tan x = \frac{\sin x}{\cos x}$
- ∴ tan x is undefined whenever cos x = 0
- the zeros of the function y = cos x become the vertical asymptotes of the function y = tan x
- y = tanx

1. period: π
2. range: y ∈ R
3. vertical asymptotes: $x = \frac{\pi}{2} + k\pi$ for all k ∈ Z

   - general tangent function: $y = a\tan(b(x - c)) + d$ where a ≠ 0, b > 0
   - principal axis: y = d
   - period: $\frac{\pi}{b}$
   - amplitude is undefined
   - there are an infinite number of vertical asymptotes

Reciprocal trigonometric functions

$\operatorname{cosec} x = \dfrac{1}{\sin x}$

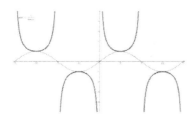

$y = \dfrac{1}{\sin x}$

$y = \sin x$

$\operatorname{secant} x = \dfrac{1}{\cos x}$

$$y = \frac{1}{\cos x}$$

$$y = \cos x$$

cotangent x = $\frac{1}{\tan x}$

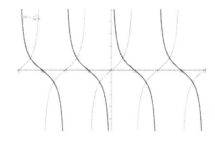

$$y = \frac{1}{\tan x}$$

$$y = \tan x$$

Inverse trigonometric functions

- used to find the angle that results in a trigonometric ratio
- represented as $\sin^{-1} x$, $\cos^{-1} x$, and $\tan^{-1} x$ OR $arcsin\ x, arccos\ x, and\ arctan\ x$

e.g. if $tan\theta = ¾$

$$\theta = tan^{-1}\left(\frac{3}{4}\right) \approx 0.644c$$

- $y = \sin x, y = \cos x, and\ y = \tan x$ are many to one functions.
- ∴ their domain has to be restricted so that they can have inverse functions

$y = \arcsin x\ or\ \sin^{-1} x$

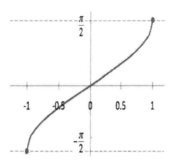

Properties

- $x = \sin y$
- domain: $-1 \leq x \leq 1$
- range: $\frac{-\pi}{2} \leq y \leq \frac{\pi}{2}$

$y = \arccos x$

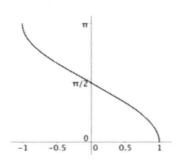

Properties

- $x = \cos y$
- domain: $-1 \leq x \leq 1$
- range: $0 \leq y \leq \pi$

$y = \arctan x$

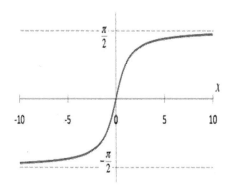

Properties

- $x = \tan y$
- domain: $x \in R$
- range: $-\frac{\pi}{2} < y < \frac{\pi}{2}$

Trigonometric equations and identities

- $\sin^2 x + \cos^2 x = 1$
- $\tan x = \frac{\sin x}{\cos x}$
- $\tan^2 x + 1 = \sec^2 x$
- $1 + \cot^2 x = \csc^2 x$

Double angle formulae

True for all angles 'x':

$$\sin 2x = 2\sin x \cos x$$

$$\cos 2x = \cos 2x - \sin 2x$$
$$= 1 - 2\sin^2 x$$
$$= 2\cos^2 x - 1$$

$$\tan 2x = \frac{2\tan x}{1 - \tan^2 x}$$

Compound angle formulae

Let A and B be any two angles:

$\cos(A \pm B) = \cos A \cos B \mp \sin A \sin B$

$\sin(A \pm B) = \sin A \cos B \pm \cos A \sin B$

$$\tan(A \pm B) = \frac{\tan A \pm \tan B}{1 \mp \tan A \tan B}$$

Product to sum formulae

$$2\sin A\cos B = \sin(A + B) + \sin(A - B)$$

$$2\cos A\cos B = \cos(A + B) + \cos(A - B)$$

$$2\sin A\sin B = \cos(A - B) - \cos(A + B)$$

Factor formulae

$$\sin A + \sin B = 2\sin\left(\frac{A + B}{2}\right)\cos\left(\frac{A - B}{2}\right)$$

$$\sin A - \sin B = 2\cos\left(\frac{A + B}{2}\right)\sin\left(\frac{A - B}{2}\right)$$

$$\cos A + \cos B = 2\cos\left(\frac{A + B}{2}\right)\cos\left(\frac{A - B}{2}\right)$$

$$\cos A - \cos B = -2\sin\left(\frac{A + B}{2}\right)\sin\left(\frac{A - B}{2}\right)$$

These formulae can be used to find solutions to trigonometric equations

Solved example:

Solve $\tan x + \sqrt{3} = 0$ for $0 < x < 4\pi$.

rearrange the equation to $\tan x = -\sqrt{3}$ and then identify the points on the unit circle with tangent $-\sqrt{3}$
i.e. $\frac{2\pi}{3}, \frac{5\pi}{3}$

after this, find all the possible solutions in the specified domain by starting and angle 0 and working around the unit circle until 4π

$$x = \frac{2\pi}{3}, \frac{5\pi}{3}, \frac{8\pi}{3}, \frac{11\pi}{3}$$

Practice time!

1. Show that $\tan\theta = \dfrac{\sin 2\theta}{1+\cos 2\theta}$

2. The radius of the circle with center O is 9.5 cm and the radius of the circle with centre P has a radius of 3.2 cm. Find the area of the shaded region id the angle AOB is $\dfrac{\pi}{3}$ and angle APB is $\dfrac{\pi}{4}$.

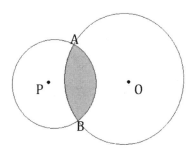

3. Find the value of $\arctan\left(\dfrac{1}{\sqrt{3}}\right) + \arctan(\sqrt{2})$ in radians.

4. Sketch the curve $f(x) = 2\cos x \sin x$ for the range $-\pi \leq x \leq \pi$.

5. $\cos 3\theta = \dfrac{4}{5}$, find the values of θ in the range $0 \leq x \leq 2\pi$.

6. Find the exact value of $\sin 150°$

7. In a triangle ABC where AB=6cm and BC=7cm and the angle B is 55° find the value of AC

8. Given that $\cos\theta = t$ for $0 \leq \theta \leq \dfrac{\pi}{2}$, find the value of $\tan\theta$ in terms of k

9. Prove that $\csc 2x = \cot x - \cot 2x$

10. Sketch the graph of $y = 2\cos\left(x - \dfrac{\pi}{5}\right)$ from $-2\pi \leq x \leq 2\pi$.

11. Prove that $\arcsin\left(\dfrac{4}{5}\right) + \arcsin\left(\dfrac{-4}{5}\right) = 0$

FUNCTIONS

2.1 Concept of function $f: x \to f(x)$: domain, range; image (value).
Odd and even functions.
Composite functions $f \circ g$.
Identity function
One-to-one and many-to-one functions.
Inverse function f^{-1}, including domain restriction.
Self-inverse functions.

2.2 The graph of a function; its equation $y = f(x)$.
Investigation of key features of graphs, such as maximum and minimum values, intercepts, horizontal and vertical asymptotes and symmetry, and consideration of domain and range.
The graphs of the functions $y = f(x)$ and $y = f(x)$.
The graph of $y = \dfrac{1}{f(x)}$ given the graph of $y = f(x)$.

2.3 Transformations of graphs: translations; stretches; reflections in the axes.
The graph of the inverse function as a reflection in $y = x$

2.4
The rational function $\dfrac{ax+b}{cx+d}$ and its graph.
The reciprocal function is a particular case.
Graphs should include both asymptotes and any intercepts with axes.
The function $x \to a^x$, $a > 0$, and its graph.
The function $x \to \log_a x$, $x > 0$, and its graph

What is a function?

It is a 'device' which will process an input into an output. Let x be our input, $f(x)$ be our 'device' and y be the output. So $f(x)$ processes our input x to produce an output y.

For example:

Let $f(x) = 3x+4$

Let $x = 2$

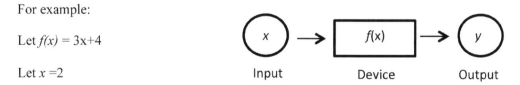

Input   Device   Output

By substituting $x = 2$ in $f(x)$ we get our y value or the output value. $3 \times (2) + 4 = 10$ and so 10 is the y value or the output value.

What is the domain of a function?

It is the input value or *x value* for which a function is defined.

For example:
For the function $f(x) = \frac{2}{x+1}$, the function holds true for any real value of *x* except for *x*= -1. At *x*= -1, the *y value* is undefined. $f(-1) \frac{2}{-1+1} = \frac{2}{0}$ this is undefined.

Solved example

Let $f(x) = \frac{4-x^2}{9-\sqrt{x}}$. State the domain for f(x)

Answer:

Just look at the denominator when the function is a fraction unless the numerator has $\sqrt{x}$. if the numerator does have a $\sqrt{x}$ then it plays a role in the decision of the domain of a function. This is called the **implied domain** as the domain is not explicitly stated but in this case we know x has to be positive, otherwise the function would be invalid.

In this case it does not. So only focus on the denominator. Now think for what value of x I will get 0 in the denominator.

$9 - \sqrt{x} = 0$

$9 = \sqrt{x}$

$X = 9^2$

What is the range of a function?

The range of a function is the output or *y value* for all x values that are defined for the function.

For Example:

Let $f(x) = 5x + 2$

Here the range of the function is all real numbers as the domain of the function is all real numbers without any exceptions.

Solved example

Let $f(x) = 3x + 2$, where x ≠ 2. State the range for f(x)

Here the range of the function is all real numbers as the domain of the function is all real numbers without any exceptions.

Solved example

Let $f(x) = 3x + 2$, where $x \neq 2$. State the range for $f(x)$

Answer:

Find the domain of the function first in case there are any exceptions. If so then these exceptions must be accounted for while calculating the range. In this case the domain is given. Now substitute the value of x for which the function is invalid in this case it is x=2.

$3(2) + 2 = 8$

So the range of this function becomes y = all real numbers except y=8.

Cartesian plane

This plane is formed through the intersection of the x-axis and the y-axis dividing the plane into four quadrants. Each point on this plane is represented by an ordered pair (x , y) where x and y denote the coordinates of the point.

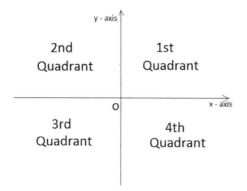

Odd functions:

When $f(x) = -f(-x)$, the function is considered to be an odd function.

For example:

$f(x) = \dfrac{x}{(x^2 - 1)}$, find out if the function is odd.

Substitute x with –x and put a negative sign to the left of the equation.

So $-f(-x) = -\dfrac{-x}{((-x)^2 - 1)}$ which is equivalent to $\dfrac{x}{(x^2 - 1)}$. Hence it is an odd function.

Even functions:

When $f(x) = f(-x)$, the functions is considered to be an even function.

If you were to plot a graph of an even function it would be symmetrical with respect to the y-axis

For example:

$f(x) = x^2$, find out if the function is even

Substitute x with –x to check if the function is even.

$(-x)^2 = x^2$ and so $f(x) = f(-x)$ therefore making this function an even function.

Composite functions:

This is when you apply the results of one function to another function

Let $f(x)$ be one function and let $g(x)$ be another.

If $f(x) = 2x+5$ and $g(x) = \frac{3}{x}$ what is f(g(x)) or (f o g)(x). Which means the y value of the function g(x) becomes the new x value of the function f(x).

take the same functions mentioned above. You are asked to find f(g(3)) or (f o g)(3).

First substitute 3 in the function g(x) to obtain a y-value. $g(3)$ is $\frac{3}{3} = 1$. Now substitute this y value in f(x). so now we find f(1) which is 2(1)+5 = 7.

Solved example

Let $f(x) = 2x + 3$

Let $g(x) = \frac{1}{x}$, $x \neq 0$

Find $(g \circ f)(x)$

Answer:

This can be translated as g of f of x. Which means the y value obtained from the function f(x) is the input in the function g(x).

$(g \circ f)(x)$ Therefore becomes $\frac{1}{2x+3}$.

As $f(x) = 2x + 3$

Let $g(x) = \dfrac{1}{x}$

Continuity

A graph is said to be continuous if there are no breaks in the graph. If there are breaks, these functions are called discontinuous functions.

Most asymptotic functions are discontinuous. Other functions are discontinuous only because of the domain that is provided.

The identity function

it is a y = x graph. Which means input equals output, the 'device' or function doesn't process it.

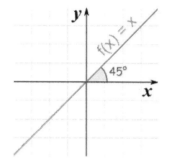

And remember the slope is always 1.

One to one function and many to one function

One to one function is a function for which the y value (output) corresponds to only one x value (input).

Inverse functions

An inverse function is denoted by $f^{-1}(x)$

On a graph $f^{-1}(x)$ is a reflection of $f(x)$ on the y=x line.

To find the inverse of a function make x the subject of the original function

For example:

A function f is defined by $f(x) = \dfrac{2x-3}{x-1}$, $x \neq 1$. Find an expression for $f^{-1}(x)$.

Let's rewrite this as $y = \dfrac{2x-3}{x-1}$

Now change the subject of the equation to x

$$y(x-1) = 2x - 3$$
$$yx - 2x = y - 3$$
$$x(y-2) = y - 3$$
$$x = \frac{y-3}{y-2}$$

as y =x , substitiute y with x to find the inverse function.

$$\Rightarrow f^{-1}(x) = \frac{x-3}{x-2} \text{ where } x \neq 2$$

Note – the range of a function is the domain of its inverse and the domain of a function acts as the range of its inverse.

Self-inverse functions

When an element combines with itself to produce the identity function it is called a self-inverse function. When $f(f(x)) = x$.

For example:

$f(x) = \frac{8}{x}$. verify if this function is a self-inverse function.

It is known that for a self-inverse function $f(f(x)) = x$. check if this condition holds true for the function above.

$\frac{8}{\frac{8}{x}} = x$. so this function is a self-inverse function.

Basic structures of a graph

Maximum – as the name suggests it is the maximum point on a graph this usually occurs when the graph is in the form $-ax^2 + bx + c$. where a is **negative**.

Minimum – it is the minimum point on the graph which occurs when the graph is in the form $ax^2 + bx + c$ where a is **positive.**

Intercept – it is the point/points where a graph cuts the x axis or the y axis. In a graph whose f(x) is a 2 degree polynomial or higher the x intercepts are the roots (solutions) of the graph.

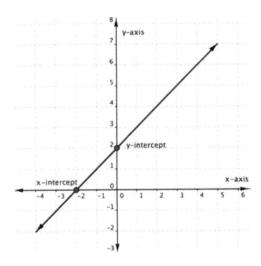

Axis of symmetry - the line about which a given graph is symmetrical. Not all graphs have an axis of symmetry.

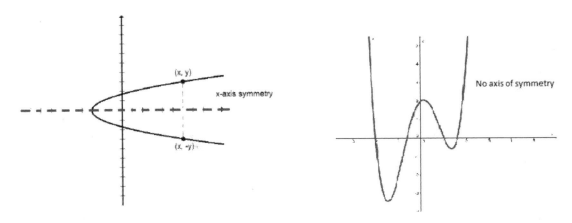

Asymptotes – It is a **line** that a curve approaches, as the curve approaches infinity.

Let us graph $f(x) = \dfrac{1}{x^2-16}$, before which you should find the domain.

In this case $x^2 - 16$ cannot be equal to zero as the function would be undefined at this point. So

$x \neq \pm 4$. These are the equations of the lines for which the function approaches infinity. And voila! These are your asymptotes. In this case you have vertical asymptotes but there are also horizontal and oblique asymptotes which are slanted asymptotes formed because y does not correspond to a constant like y=2 but rather to another variable like y=x. so the asymptote is a slanted line.

The modulus function-

These graphs will not have a negative y value for any x value and has a V-shape.

For example

Let $|f(x)| = |x + 5|$

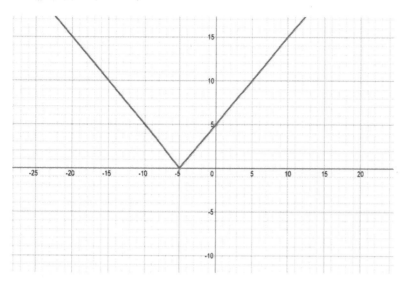

The basic modulus functions as the one above is very simple but you might also encounter other problems such as

$f(|x|) = |x| - 3$

Over here the modulus applies to only the x value not the function as a whole.

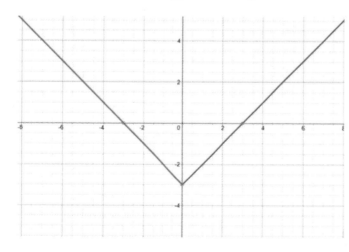

If such questions appear in paper 1 (no calculator) do modulus of x and then bring it down or up by the number outside of the modulus. In this case it is -3 so it is moved down by 3 units

Exponential functions-

Its of the form $f(x) = a^x$ where **a** is any constant.

For eg:

Let $f(x) = 2^x$. The graph would look like this

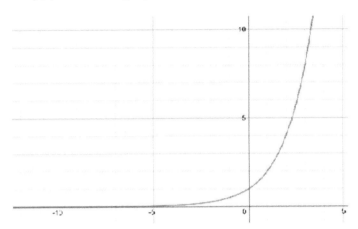

All exponential tends to infinity. The domain is $(-\infty, \infty)$ and the range is always positive $y > 0$. as **a** is always positive. The asymptote here is x- axis

If $f(x) = 2^x - 7$. The graph would look a little different.

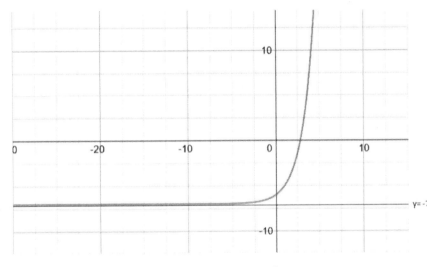

The graph 2^x has shifted down by 7 units for the graph of $2^x - 7$. If the exponent is followed by a constant, in this case -7, it is shifted up or down by that many units

Now if we had another function $f(x) = 2^{x+2}$. It would move to the left by k units. when the constant accompanying x in the power is positive it moves to the left and if the constant is negative it moves to the right. As shown below

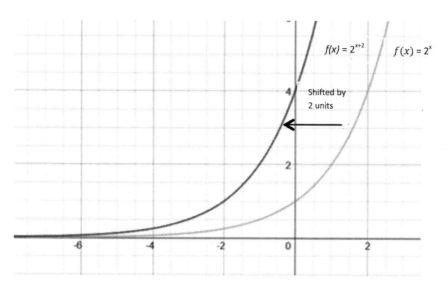

Logarithmic functions-

For eg:

Let $f(x) = \log_2(3x - 2)$, the graph would look like this:

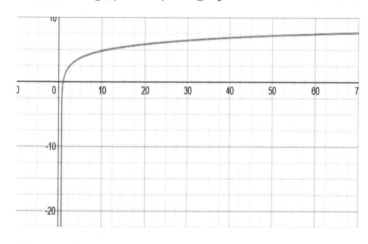

The same rules apply to logarithmic functions as they do to exponents. If there is a constant, a, outside the log function- the graph moves up or down by *a* units. If a constant, *k is* added to x inside the logarithm function it moves left or right by *k* units.

The graph of $y = k \times a^x, k > 0$ is identical to $y = a^x$ but

- Stretched along the y-axis if $k > 1$
- Shrunk along the y-axis if $0 < k < 1$

The graph of $y = k \times a^x, k < 0$ is identical to $y = a^x$ but

1 Reflected about the x-axis and stretched along the y-axis if $k < -1$.

   a) Reflected about the x-axis and shrunk along the y-axis if $-1 < k < 0$.

Practise time!

1. Let $f(x) = \sqrt{\dfrac{1}{(x-2)^2} - 4}$. Find

   (a) the set of real values of x for which f is real and finite;
   (b) the range of f.

2. The function $f(x) = \dfrac{3x-2}{2x+4}$, x ∈ R, x ≠ -2. Find the inverse function, f^{-1}, clearly stating its domain.

3. The functions f(x) and g(x) are given by $f(x) = \sqrt{2x-3}$ and $g(x) = x^2 + 2x + 1$. The function (fog)(x) is defined for x ∈ R, except for the interval (a,b).

   (a) Calculate values of a and b.
   (b) Find the range of fog.

4. Find the exact value of x satisfying the equation

   $$5^{2x+1} \cdot 7^x = 35^{x+1}.$$

   Give your answer in the form $\dfrac{\ln a}{\ln b}$ where a, b ∈ Z.

5. Find range of values of m such that $m(2x+1) \leq 3x^2$.

6. Solve the equation $\log_3(x-4) + \log_{\frac{1}{9}} \dfrac{1}{\sqrt{x-2}} = 3$.

7. Solve the equation $3^{2(x+1)} = 82.3^{2x} - 9$.

8. The graph of the function $f(x) = x^3 + 2x^2 - 3x + 1$ is translated to its image, g(x), by the vector $\begin{pmatrix} 2 \\ -1 \end{pmatrix}$. Write g(x) in the form $g(x) = ax^3 + bx^2 + cx + d$.

9. (a) Express the quadratic function $y = 2x^2 - 4x + 7$ in the form $a(x+b)^2 + c$, where a, b, c ∈ Z.

   (b) Describe a sequence of transformations that transforms the graph of $y = x^2$ to the graph of

   $y = 2x^2 - 4x + 7$.

10. Shown below are the graphs of y = f(x) and y = g(x).

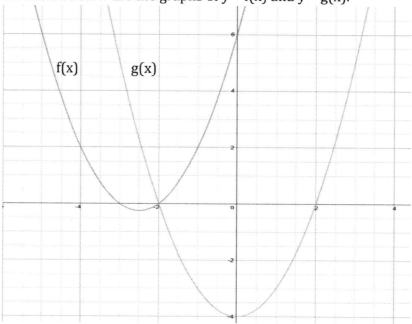

If (fog)(x) = 6, find all possible values of x.

VECTORS

4.1 Concept of a vector.
Representation of vectors using directed line segments.
Unit vectors; base vectors *i, j, k*.
$$v = \begin{pmatrix} v_1 \\ v_2 \\ v_3 \end{pmatrix} = v_1 i + v_2 j + v_3 k$$
Algebraic and geometric approaches to the following:
• the sum and difference of two vectors;
• the zero vector **0**, the vector $-v$;
• multiplication by a scalar, kv;
• magnitude of a vector, v;
• position vectors OA= *a*.
AB= *b* – *a*

4.2 The definition of the scalar product of two vectors.
Properties of the scalar product:
$v \cdot w = w \cdot v$;
$u \cdot (v + w) = u \cdot v + u \cdot w$;
$(kv) \cdot w = k(v \cdot w)$;
$v \cdot v = |v|^2$
The angle between two vectors.
Perpendicular vectors; parallel vectors.

4.3 Vector equation of a line in two and three dimensions: $r = a + \lambda b$.
Simple applications to kinematics.
The angle between two lines.

4.4 Coincident, parallel, intersecting and skew lines; distinguishing between these cases.
Points of intersection.

4.5 The definition of the vector product of two vectors.
Properties of the vector product:
$v \times w = -w \times v$;
$u \times (v + w) = u \times v + u \times w$;
$(kv) \times w = k(v \times w)$;
$v \times v = 0$.

4.6 Vector equation of a plane $r = a + \lambda b + \mu c$.
Use of normal vector to obtain the form
$r \cdot n = a \cdot n$.
Cartesian equation of a plane $ax + by + cz = d$.

4.7 Intersections of: a line with a plane; two planes; three planes.
Angle between: a line and a plane; two planes

1. length of arrow = magnitude of the quantity
2. arrowhead = direction
3. e.g. the diagram opposite shows velocity = 30 m/s to the northeast (bearing of 045°)

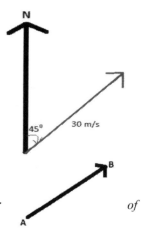

- position vector
- if $\overrightarrow{OA}$ is a vector from origin O to point A, it is the position vector of point A
- representations: $\overrightarrow{OA}, \vec{a}, \bar{a}, \mathbf{a}$
- magnitude of $\overrightarrow{OA}$ = $|\overrightarrow{OA}|$, OA, $|\mathbf{a}|$, $|\bar{a}|$, $|\vec{a}|$
- if $\overrightarrow{AB}$ is a vector from point A to B, then it is the position vector of point B relative to point A
- geometric vector equality
  • 2 vectors are equal if they have the same magnitude and direction
  • properties of equal vectors – parallel, in the same direction, equal in length
  • the arrows representing equal vectors are translations of one another
  • equal vectors are free vectors: a vector with a given magnitude and direction can be drawn from any point
- geometric negative vectors
  • vectors $\overrightarrow{AB}$ and $\overrightarrow{BA}$ have the same length but opposite directions, so they are negatives of one another
  • i.e. $\overrightarrow{BA} = -\overrightarrow{AB}$

Geometric Operations with vectors

	Explanation
Geometric vector addition	Geometric definition of vector **a + b**: - draw **a** - at the arrowhead of **a** draw **b** - the vector from the beginning of **a** to the arrowhead of **b** is the vector **a + b** Zero vector ($\vec{0}$): *vector of length 0* for any vector **a**, $a + 0 = 0 + a = a$ $a + (-a) = (-a) + a = 0$

Geometric vector subtraction	Concept: *to subtract one vector from another, add its negative* *i.e.* ***a** – **b** = **a** + (-**b**)*	
Vector equations	Concept: *when there are vectors forming a closed polygon, vector equations can be used to relate the variables* *i.e. select any vector for the LHS and trace the path from its starting point to its arrowhead*	
Geometric scalar multiplication	Concept: *if **a** is a vector and 'k' is a scalar, then k**a** is also a vector* - *if $k > 0$, k**a** and **a** have the same direction* - *if $k < 0$, k**a** and **a** have opposite directions* - *if $k = 0$, k**a** = 0 and it is a zero vector* -	

Vectors in the plane

- *position vectors*
    - *the point $P(x, y)$ has position vector $\overrightarrow{OP} = \begin{pmatrix} x \\ y \end{pmatrix} = x\mathbf{i} + y\mathbf{j}$*
    - *representations: the component vector form $\begin{pmatrix} x \\ y \end{pmatrix}$ or the unit vector form $x\mathbf{i} + y\mathbf{j}$*
    - *all vectors in the plane can be described in terms of base unit vectors $\mathbf{i}$ and $\mathbf{j}$*
- *unit vectors*
    - *definition: vectors with a magnitude of 1 unit*
    - *$\mathbf{i} = \begin{pmatrix} 1 \\ 0 \end{pmatrix}$ is the base unit vector in the positive x-direction*
    - *$\mathbf{j} = \begin{pmatrix} 0 \\ 1 \end{pmatrix}$ is the base unit vector in the positive y-direction*
    - *the set of vectors $\{\mathbf{i}, \mathbf{j}\} = \{\begin{pmatrix} 1 \\ 0 \end{pmatrix}, \begin{pmatrix} 0 \\ 1 \end{pmatrix}\}$ is the basis for the 2-D (x, y) coordinate system*
- *equal vectors: 2 vectors are equal if their $\mathbf{i}$ and $\mathbf{j}$ components are equal*

Example: *Write $\overrightarrow{OA}$ and $\overrightarrow{CB}$ in component form and unit vector form.*

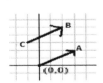

$\overrightarrow{OA} = \begin{pmatrix} 3 \\ 2 \end{pmatrix} = 3i + 2j$

Magnitude of a vector

1. if $\mathbf{a} = \begin{pmatrix} a_1 \\ a_2 \end{pmatrix} = a_1 \mathbf{i} + a_2 \mathbf{j}$, the magnitude or length of $\mathbf{a}$ is $|\mathbf{a}| = \sqrt{a_1^2 + a_2^2}$
2. explanation: this formula is derived from Pythagoras' theorem, as shown in the diagram

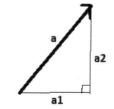

Operations with plane vectors

	Explanation	Example
Algebraic vector addition	If $\mathbf{a} = \begin{pmatrix} a_1 \\ a_2 \end{pmatrix}$ and $\mathbf{b} = \begin{pmatrix} b_1 \\ b_2 \end{pmatrix}$ then $\mathbf{a} + \mathbf{b} = \begin{pmatrix} a_1+b_1 \\ a_2+b_2 \end{pmatrix}$	If $\mathbf{a} = \begin{pmatrix} 2 \\ -2 \end{pmatrix}$ and $\mathbf{b} = \begin{pmatrix} 3 \\ 5 \end{pmatrix}$, find $\mathbf{a} + \mathbf{b}$. Check your answer graphically. $\mathbf{a} + \mathbf{b} = \begin{pmatrix} 2+3 \\ -2+5 \end{pmatrix} = \begin{pmatrix} 5 \\ 3 \end{pmatrix}$
Algebraic negative vectors	If $\mathbf{a} = \begin{pmatrix} a_1 \\ a_2 \end{pmatrix}$ and $-\mathbf{a} = \begin{pmatrix} -a_1 \\ -a_2 \end{pmatrix}$	
Algebraic vector subtraction	If $\mathbf{a} = \begin{pmatrix} a_1 \\ a_2 \end{pmatrix}$ and $\mathbf{b} = \begin{pmatrix} b_1 \\ b_2 \end{pmatrix}$ then $\mathbf{a} - \mathbf{b} = \begin{pmatrix} a_1-b_1 \\ a_2-b_2 \end{pmatrix}$ Concept: to subtract one vector from another, add its negative i.e. $\mathbf{a} - \mathbf{b} = \mathbf{a} + (-\mathbf{b})$	Given $\mathbf{a} = \begin{pmatrix} 2 \\ -5 \end{pmatrix}$ and $\mathbf{b} = \begin{pmatrix} -9 \\ 1 \end{pmatrix}$ and $\mathbf{c} = \begin{pmatrix} 6 \\ 3 \end{pmatrix}$, find $\mathbf{a} - \mathbf{b} - \mathbf{c}$. $\mathbf{a} - \mathbf{b} - \mathbf{c}$ $= \begin{pmatrix} 2 \\ -5 \end{pmatrix} - \begin{pmatrix} -9 \\ 1 \end{pmatrix} - \begin{pmatrix} 6 \\ 3 \end{pmatrix}$ $= \begin{pmatrix} 2 \\ -5 \end{pmatrix} + \begin{pmatrix} 9 \\ -1 \end{pmatrix} + \begin{pmatrix} -6 \\ -3 \end{pmatrix}$ $= \begin{pmatrix} 5 \\ -9 \end{pmatrix}$

| Algebraic scalar multiplication | If 'k' is any scalar and $a = \begin{pmatrix} a_1 \\ a_2 \end{pmatrix}$, then $ka = \begin{pmatrix} ka_1 \\ ka_2 \end{pmatrix}$.

- if $k = -1$, $ka = (-1)a = -a$
- if $k = 0$, $ka = (0)a = 0$ | Given $a = \begin{pmatrix} 2 \\ -5 \end{pmatrix}$ and $b = \begin{pmatrix} 4 \\ 1 \end{pmatrix}$, find $a + 3b$.

$a + 3b$
$= \begin{pmatrix} 2 \\ -5 \end{pmatrix} + 3\begin{pmatrix} 4 \\ 1 \end{pmatrix}$
$= \begin{pmatrix} 2+3(4) \\ -5+3(1) \end{pmatrix}$
$= \begin{pmatrix} 14 \\ -2 \end{pmatrix}$ |

Vector between two points

1. for 2 points A and B with position vectors **a** and **b** respectively, the position vector of point B relative to point A is $\overrightarrow{AB} = \overrightarrow{OB} - \overrightarrow{OA} = b - a = \begin{pmatrix} b_1 - a_1 \\ b_2 - a_2 \end{pmatrix}$
2. magnitude of $\overrightarrow{AB}$ is $|\overrightarrow{AB}| = \sqrt{(b_1 - a_1)^2 + (b_2 - a_2)^2}$
3. example: [AB] is the diameter of a circle with center C(-1, 2). If B is (3, 1), find $\overrightarrow{BC}$ and the coordinates of A
   - $\overrightarrow{BC} = \begin{pmatrix} -1-3 \\ 2-1 \end{pmatrix} = \begin{pmatrix} -4 \\ 1 \end{pmatrix}$
   - Let A have coordinates (a,b)

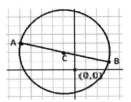

$$\overrightarrow{CA} = \begin{pmatrix} a - (-1) \\ b - 2 \end{pmatrix} = \begin{pmatrix} a + 1 \\ b - 2 \end{pmatrix}$$

$$\overrightarrow{CA} = \overrightarrow{BC}, so \begin{pmatrix} a + 1 \\ b - 2 \end{pmatrix} = \begin{pmatrix} -4 \\ 1 \end{pmatrix}$$

$$\therefore a + 1 = -4, a = -5$$

$$b - 2 = 1, b = 3$$

So A is $(-5, 3)$

Vectors in space

Concepts	Operations
Introduction:	Introduction:
— rigin (O): point of reference to specify points in 3-D space	the rules for algebra with vectors in 2-D can be applied to vectors in 3-D

- X, Y, and Z-axes: mutually perpendicular lines drawn through O - any point P in space can be specified by an ordered triple of numbers (x, y, z) where x, y, and z are steps in the X, Y, and Z directions from the origin O to P	- if $a = \begin{pmatrix} a_1 \\ a_2 \\ a_3 \end{pmatrix}$ and $b = \begin{pmatrix} b_1 \\ b_2 \\ b_3 \end{pmatrix}$ then $a + b = \begin{pmatrix} a_1 + b_1 \\ a_2 + b_2 \\ a_3 + b_3 \end{pmatrix}$ and $a - b = \begin{pmatrix} a_1 - b_1 \\ a_2 - b_2 \\ a_3 - b_3 \end{pmatrix}$ - $ka = \begin{pmatrix} ka_1 \\ ka_2 \\ ka_3 \end{pmatrix}$ for any scalar 'k'
Position Vector: - position vector of $P = \overrightarrow{OP} = \begin{pmatrix} x \\ y \\ z \end{pmatrix} = x\mathbf{i} + y\mathbf{j} + z\mathbf{k}$ - $\mathbf{i} = \begin{pmatrix} 1 \\ 0 \\ 0 \end{pmatrix}, \mathbf{j} = \begin{pmatrix} 0 \\ 1 \\ 0 \end{pmatrix}, \mathbf{k} = \begin{pmatrix} 0 \\ 0 \\ 1 \end{pmatrix}$ are base unit vectors in the X, Y, and Z directions respectively - the set of vectors $\{\mathbf{i}, \mathbf{j}, \mathbf{k}\} = \left\{\begin{pmatrix} 1 \\ 0 \\ 0 \end{pmatrix}, \begin{pmatrix} 0 \\ 1 \\ 0 \end{pmatrix}, \begin{pmatrix} 0 \\ 0 \\ 1 \end{pmatrix}\right\}$ is the basis for the 3-D (x, y, z) coordinate system	**Properties of Vectors in space:** - commutative property: $a + b = b + a$ - associative property: $(a + b) + c = a + (b + c)$ - additive identity: $a + 0 = 0 + a = a$ - additive inverse: $a + (-a) = (-a) + a = 0$ - distributive property: $k(a+b) = ka + kb$
Magnitude of a vector: if vector $a = \begin{pmatrix} a_1 \\ a_2 \\ a_3 \end{pmatrix}$, the magnitude of a is $\|a\| = \sqrt{a_1^2 + a_2^2 + a_3^2}$	**Length of vector ka:** $\|ka\| = \|k\|\|a\|$ where ka is parallel to a
Vector between 2 points: let $A(x_1, y_1, z_1)$ and $B(x_2, y_2, z_2)$ be 2 points in space	**Rules and proof:** - if $x + a = b$ then $x = b - a$ if $x + a = b$

Vector equality:	
- if $a = \begin{pmatrix} a_1 \\ a_2 \\ a_3 \end{pmatrix}$ and $b = \begin{pmatrix} b_1 \\ b_2 \\ b_3 \end{pmatrix}$, then $a = b$ $\Leftrightarrow a_1 = b_1, a_2 = b_2, a_3 = b_3$ - if a and b do not coincide, then they are opposite sides of a parallelogram and lie in the same plane	

Parallelism

1. **parallel vectors**
   - if a is parallel to b, then there is a scalar 'k' such that $a = kb$
   - e.g. a, ½ a, and $3a$ are parallel vectors
   - if $a = kb$ for a scalar 'k', then $a \parallel b$ and $|a| = |k||b|$

2. **unit vectors**
   - a unit vector in the direction of vector a is $\frac{1}{|a|}a$ ($|a|$ is a scalar quantity)
   - a vector b of length 'k' in the <u>same direction as</u> a is $b = \frac{k}{|a|}a$
   - a vector b of length 'k' that is <u>parallel to</u> a is $b = \pm\frac{k}{|a|}a$

3. **collinear points**
   - 3 or more points are collinear if they lie on the same straight line
   - A, B, and C are collinear if $\overrightarrow{AB} = k\overrightarrow{BC}$ for some scalar 'k'

* $|k|$ is the modulus of 'k', but $|a|$ is the magnitude of a vector a

Scalar and vector product of two vectors

Scalar product	Vector product
Introduction: - also called dot product - results in a scalar answer - notation: $a \cdot b$ (*a dot b*)	Introduction: 1. also called cross product 2. results in a vector answer 3. notation: $a \times b$ (*a cross b*) 4. used to find a vector which is perpendicular to two other known vectors 5. can be used to find the areas of triangles and parallelograms defined by 2 vectors

Basic concept:	Basic concept:
if $a = \begin{pmatrix} a_1 \\ a_2 \\ a_3 \end{pmatrix}$ and $b = \begin{pmatrix} b_1 \\ b_2 \\ b_3 \end{pmatrix}$, the scalar product of **a** and **b** is defined as $$a \cdot b = a_1b_1 + a_2b_2 + a_3b_3$$	if $a = \begin{pmatrix} a_1 \\ a_2 \\ a_3 \end{pmatrix}$ and $b = \begin{pmatrix} b_1 \\ b_2 \\ b_3 \end{pmatrix}$, the vector cross product of **a** and **b** is defined as $$a \times b = \begin{pmatrix} a_2b_3 - a_3b_2 \\ a_3b_1 - a_1b_3 \\ a_1b_2 - a_2b_1 \end{pmatrix}$$ alternative formula: $$a \times b = \begin{vmatrix} i & j & k \\ a_1 & a_2 & a_3 \\ b_1 & b_2 & b_3 \end{vmatrix}$$ $$= \begin{vmatrix} a_2 & a_3 \\ b_2 & b_3 \end{vmatrix} i - \begin{vmatrix} a_1 & a_3 \\ b_1 & b_3 \end{vmatrix} j + \begin{vmatrix} a_1 & a_2 \\ b_1 & b_2 \end{vmatrix}$$ where $\begin{vmatrix} a_2 & a_3 \\ b_2 & b_3 \end{vmatrix} = (a_2b_3 - a_3b_2)$ → product of major diagonal — product of minor diagonal $$\therefore a \times b = (a_2b_3 - a_3b_2)i - (a_1b_3 - a_3b_1)j + (a_1b_2 - a_2b_1)k$$
<u>Application</u>: angle between vectors	<u>Application</u>: length of $a \times b$
Consider vectors $a = \begin{pmatrix} a_1 \\ a_2 \\ a_3 \end{pmatrix}$ and $b = \begin{pmatrix} b_1 \\ b_2 \\ b_3 \end{pmatrix}$ in the diagram. The angle between vectors is always taken such that $0° \leq \Theta \leq 180°$. Using cosine rule	Let Θ be the angle between **a** and **b**. length of $a \times b$ is $\|a \times b\| = \|a\|\|b\| \sin\Theta$ Proof: $\|a\|^2\|b\|^2 \sin^2\Theta$ $= \|a\|^2\|b\|^2(1-\cos^2\Theta)$ $= \|a\|^2\|b\|^2 - \|a\|^2\|b\|^2\cos^2\Theta$

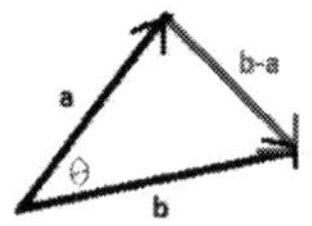

$\|b-a\|^2 = \|a\|^2 + \|b\|^2 - 2\|a\|\|b\|\cos\theta$ $b - a = \begin{pmatrix} b_1 - a_1 \\ b_2 - a_2 \\ b_3 - a_3 \end{pmatrix}$ $\therefore (b_1 - a_1)^2 + (b_2 - a_2)^2 + (b_3 - a_3)^2$ $= a_1^2 + a_2^2 + a_3^2 + b_1^2 + b_2^2 + b_3^2 - 2\|a\|\|b\|\cos\theta$ $\therefore a_1 b_1 + a_2 b_2 + a_3 b_3 = \|a\|\|b\|\cos\theta$ $\therefore a \cdot b = \|a\|\|b\|\cos\theta$ So the angle θ between 2 vectors can be found using the formula $\cos\theta = \dfrac{a \cdot b}{\|a\|\|b\|}$ - if $\theta < 90^0$, $\cos\theta > 0$, so $a \cdot b > 0$ - if $\theta > 90^0$, $\cos\theta < 0$, so $a \cdot b < 0$	$= \|a\|^2\|b\|^2 - (a \cdot b)^2$ $= (a_1^2 + a_2^2 + a_3^2)(b_1^2 + b_2^2 + b_3^2) - (a_1 b_1 + a_2 b_2 + a_3 b_3)^2$. expand and factorise $= (a_2 b_3 - a_3 b_2)^2 + (a_3 b_1 - a_1 b_3)^2 + (a_1 b_2 - a_2 b_1)^2$ $= \| a \times b \|^2$ $\therefore \| a \times b \| = \|a\|\|b\| \sin\theta$ (as $\sin\theta > 0$)
Algebraic properties: - $a \cdot b = b \cdot a$ - $a \cdot a = \|a\|^2$ - $a \cdot (b + c) = a \cdot b + a \cdot c$ *scalar **product** = product of 2 vectors to give a scalar answer, whereas scalar **multiplication** = product of a scalar and a vector to give a parallel vector - $(a + b) \cdot (c + d) = a \cdot c + a \cdot d + b \cdot c + b \cdot d$	Algebraic properties: 1. $a \times b$ is a vector perpendicular to a and b *i.e. $a \times b$ and $b \times a$ have same length but opp direction 2. $a \times a = 0$ for all a 3. $a \times b = -b \times a$ for all a and b 4. $a \cdot (b \times c)$ is called scalar triple product 5. $a \times (b + c) = (a \times b) + (a \times c)$ 6. $(a + b) \times (c + d) = (a \times c) + (a \times d) + (b \times c) + (b \times d)$

Geometric properties:		Geometric properties:	
- for non-zero vectors **a** and **b**, **a** • **b** = 0 ⇔ **a** and **b** are perpendicular - |**a** • **b**| = |**a**||**b**| ⇔ **a** and **b** are non-zero parallel vectors - if **a** is perpendicular to **b** (Θ = 90^0), $\cos\Theta$ = 0 so **a** • **b** = 0 - if **a** is parallel to **b** (Θ = 0^0 or 180^0), $\cos\Theta$ = ±1 so **a** • **b** = ± |**a**||**b**| and |**a**•**b**| = |**a**||**b**|	1 2 3 4	use the **right hand rule** to determine the direction of **a** × **b** i.e. turn fingers of the right hand from **a** to **b**, and thumb will point in the direction of **a** × **b** if **u** is a unit vector in the direction of **a** × **b** then **a** × **b** = |**a**||**b**|$\sin\theta$**u** if **a** and **b** are non-zero vectors, then **a** × **b** = 0 ⇔ **a** is parallel to **b**	

VECTOR APPLICATIONS

Problems involving vector operations

- vectors can be applied to real life situations
- resultant vector: a measure of the combined effect when vectors are added together
- e.g. the resultant vector of the forces acting on the box diagram is $F_1 + F_2$

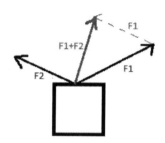

	Concept	**Formulae**
Area	Use vector cross product to find the areas of triangles and parallelograms defined by 2 vectors	- area of a triangle with defining vectors **a** and **b** is $A = \frac{1}{2}\|a \times b\|$ units^2 - area of a parallelogram with defining vectors **a** and **b** is $A = \|a \times b\|$ units^2 Proof: $\quad$ area of Δ $= \frac{1}{2} \times \text{product of 2 sides}$ $\times \text{sine of included angle}$ $\therefore A \text{ of } \Delta = \frac{1}{2}\|a\|\|b\|\sin\theta = \frac{1}{2}\|a \times b\|$ *parallelogram consists of 2 congruent triangles, so its proof follows directly from this

| Lines in 2D and 3D | 1. The equation of a line can be determined using its direction and any fixed point on the line e.g. a line passes through a fixed point A with position vector **a** and is parallel to vector **b**. Let R be a point on the line, with position vector **r**. $\overrightarrow{OR} = \overrightarrow{OA} + \overrightarrow{AR}$ $r = a + \overrightarrow{AR}$ $\overrightarrow{AR} \parallel b \therefore \overrightarrow{AR} = \lambda b, \lambda \in R$ $\therefore$ vector eqn of line: $r = a + \lambda b, \lambda \in R$

 2. The vector equation of a line is not unique
- a line with direction vector $\begin{pmatrix} -2 \\ 5 \end{pmatrix}$ can be described by any vector $k\begin{pmatrix} 2 \\ -5 \end{pmatrix}$, where k is a non-zero scalar constant
- if there is a line passing through (1,8) and (3, 3), either point can be used as the fixed point with position vector **a**
- when different fixed points are being used, different parameters have to be used as well
- e.g. for a line passing through (1, 8) and (3, 3) with direction vector $\begin{pmatrix} -2 \\ 5 \end{pmatrix}$, the equation of the line can be written as

$x = \begin{pmatrix} 1 \\ 8 \end{pmatrix} + \lambda \begin{pmatrix} -2 \\ 5 \end{pmatrix}, \lambda \in R$ | **Lines in 2D**: *line in a plane*

 1. Vector equation: $$\begin{pmatrix} x \\ y \end{pmatrix} = \begin{pmatrix} a_1 \\ a_2 \end{pmatrix} + \lambda \begin{pmatrix} b_1 \\ b_2 \end{pmatrix}$$ - R (x, y) is any point on the line
- $A(a_1, a_2)$ is a known fixed point on the line
- $b = \begin{pmatrix} b_1 \\ b_2 \end{pmatrix}$ is the direction vector of the line
- gradient of the line is $m = \frac{b_2}{b_1}$

 2. Parametric equation: $$\begin{cases} x = a_1 + \lambda b_1 \\ y = a_2 + \lambda b_2 \end{cases}$$ - $\lambda \in R$ is the parameter
- each point on the line corresponds to **one** value of λ

 3. Cartesian equation: $$\lambda = \frac{x - a_1}{b_1} = \frac{y - a_2}{b_2}$$ $\therefore b_2 x - b_1 y = b_2 a_1 - b_1 a_2$

 Lines in 3D: *line in space*

 1. Vector equation: $$\begin{pmatrix} x \\ y \\ z \end{pmatrix} = \begin{pmatrix} a_1 \\ a_2 \\ a_3 \end{pmatrix} + \lambda \begin{pmatrix} b_1 \\ b_2 \\ b_3 \end{pmatrix}$$ - R (x, y, z) is any point on the line
- $A(a_1, a_2, a_3)$ is a known fixed point on the line |

	OR $x = \begin{pmatrix} 3 \\ 3 \end{pmatrix} + \mu \begin{pmatrix} -2 \\ 5 \end{pmatrix}, \mu \in \mathbb{R}$ $\mu = 1 - \lambda$	- $b = \begin{pmatrix} b_1 \\ b_2 \\ b_3 \end{pmatrix}$ is the direction vector of the line - no gradient, as direction of a line in space is only described by its direction vector 2. Parametric equation: $x = a_1 + \lambda b_1$ $y = a_2 + \lambda b_2$ $z = a_3 + \lambda b_3$ - $\lambda \in \mathbb{R}$ is the parameter - each point on the line corresponds to **one** value of λ 3. Cartesian equation: $\lambda = \dfrac{x - a_1}{b_1} = \dfrac{y - a_2}{b_2} = \dfrac{z - a_3}{b_3}$

Angles between 2 lines	*Usually the acute angle between two lines is calculated* $\therefore \cos\theta > 0$	- for an acute angle between lines L_1 and L_2 with direction vectors b_1 and b_2 respectively:
		$\cos\theta = \dfrac{|\boldsymbol{b_1} \cdot \boldsymbol{b_2}|}{|\boldsymbol{b_1}||\boldsymbol{b_2}|}$
		
		- Consider the lines $r_1 = a_1 + \lambda b_1$ and $r_2 = a_2 + \mu b_2$
		   • $r_1 \parallel r_2$ if $b_1 = k b_2$ for some scalar 'k'
		   • $r_1 \perp r_2$ if $b_1 \cdot b_2 = 0$

Constant velocity problems	*Remember that velocity is a vector and speed is a scalar* *The parameter in these situations corresponds to time*	1. if an object has initial position vector **a** and moves with constant velocity **b**, its position at time 't' is: $r = a + tb, t \geq 0$ 2. the speed of the object $= |b|$

Shortest distance from a line to a point	*Two points are always closest when they are perpendicular to one another* *∴ the shortest distance from a line to a point = length of the perpendicular from the point to the line*	
Intersecting lines	*To find the point of intersection of 2 lines: use simultaneous equations to solve the vector equations of the two intersecting lines*	

Relationships between lines

	Line classification in 2-D	Line classification in 3-D
Introduction	*To classify lines in 2D, the equations of the lines can be solved simultaneously using "row operations"*	
Classification	Intersecting lines: - one point of intersection - unique solution Parallel lines: 1. lines do not meet 2. no solutions Coincident lines: - lines are identical - infinite solutions	Coplanar lines - lie in the same plane - may be intersecting, parallel, or coincident Skew lines - lines that do not lie in the same plane - to find a point of intersection, one line must be translated to intersect with the other - the angle between the original lines = the angle between the intersecting lines (Θ)

		Parallel lines
		- the angle between the 2 lines is $0°$
		Intersecting lines
		- the angle between 2 intersecting lines is θ
Methods to find solutions	Row operations:	Use the concepts of simultaneous equations, intersection of 2 lines and angle between two lines
	The system of equations $\begin{cases} x - 2y = 8 \\ 4x + y = 5 \end{cases}$ is called a 2 X 2 system because there are 2 equations with 2 unknowns	
	• Properties - the equations can be interchanged without affecting the solutions - an equation can be replaced by a non-zero multiple of itself $e.g. \, x - 2y = 8$	
	can be replaced by $2x - 4y = 16$ - any equation can be replaced by a multiple of itself plus/minus a multiple of another equation $e.g.$ the second equation $4x + y = 5$ can be	

replaced by

twice the second equation
− the first equation

$$8x + 2y = 10$$
$$-(x - 2y = 8)$$
_____
$$7x + 4y = 2$$

so the system becomes

$$\begin{cases} x - 2y = 8 \\ 7x + 4y = 2 \end{cases}$$

- Augmented matrices: *the coefficients are detached from the system of equations and written as an augmented matrix to allow elementary row operations*

augmented matrix =

$$\begin{pmatrix} 1 & -2 & | & 8 \\ 4 & 1 & | & 5 \end{pmatrix}$$

- Elementary row operations:
  - *includes interchanging rows, replacing a row by a non-zero multiple of itself, and replacing any row by itself plus/minus a multiple of another row*
  - *the process of solving a system using elementary row operations is called* **row reduction**

	- *aim: to perform row operations until we get an echelon matrix i.e. a matrix in which the bottom left hand corner only has zeros*	
Examples	Use row operations to solve $\begin{cases} x - 2y = 8 \\ 4x + y = 5 \end{cases}$	Find the point of intersection between the following pair of lines. Find the measure of the acute angle between them.
	Step 1: write in augmented matrix form $\begin{pmatrix} 1 & -2 & \vert & 8 \\ 4 & 1 & \vert & 5 \end{pmatrix}$	$x = 1 + 2t, y = 2 - t, z = 3 + t$ $x = -2 + 3s, y = 3 - s, z = 1 + 2s$ *Step 1: at the point of intersection, the x, y, and z values of both lines will be the same. Equate the x, y, and z values in the lines to find a system of equations in two unknowns 't' and 's', which can be solved to find the point of intersection if it exists.*
	Step 2: Perform row reduction to get an echelon matrix $row_2 = 4row_1 - row_2$ $\begin{pmatrix} 1 & -2 & \vert & 8 \\ 0 & -9 & \vert & 27 \end{pmatrix}$ *from row 2,* $-9y = 27$ $\therefore y = -3$	$1 + 2t = -2 + 3s, \therefore 3s - 2t = 3$ $2 - t = 3 - s, \therefore s - t = 1$ $3 + t = 1 + 2s, \therefore 2s - t = 2$ *Step 2: Solve the simultaneous eqns*
	Step 3: Substitute the value of y into equation 1. $x - 2(-3) = 8$ $\therefore x = 8 - 6 = 2$	*from eqn 2,* $t = s - 1$ *sub in eqn 3,* $2s - (s - 1) = 2$ $\therefore s + 1 = 2, s = 1$ $\therefore t = 0$ *Step 3: if the lines intersect when t=0 and s=1, these values must satisfy all three equations. To check this, substitute these values in eqn 1*

when $t = 0$ and $s = 1$

Step 4: Find the coordinates of the pt of intersection

Using $t = 0, x = 1, y = 2, z = 3$

$\therefore (1, 2, 3)$

Step 5: Find the direction vectors for the lines to calculate the acute angle θ between them.

Direction vectors are $\begin{pmatrix} 2 \\ -1 \\ 1 \end{pmatrix}$ and $\begin{pmatrix} 3 \\ -1 \\ 2 \end{pmatrix}$

$\cos\theta = \dfrac{\left|\begin{pmatrix} 2 \\ -1 \\ 1 \end{pmatrix} \cdot \begin{pmatrix} 3 \\ -1 \\ 2 \end{pmatrix}\right|}{\left|\begin{pmatrix} 2 \\ -1 \\ 1 \end{pmatrix}\right|\left|\begin{pmatrix} 3 \\ -1 \\ 2 \end{pmatrix}\right|}, \theta \approx \mathbf{10.9°}$

Planes

- definition: flat surface which has zero thickness and extends forever
- 2 dimensional
- a vector is parallel to a plane if we remain on the plane by travelling along the vector
- e.g. if both A and B lie on a plane then $\overrightarrow{AB}$ is parallel to the plane

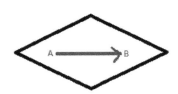

- an infinite number of planes with different orientation can be parallel to one direction vector
- to find equation of a plane: must know a point on the plane and its orientation in space
- to define orientation of a plane
  - we need 2 non-parallel vectors which are both parallel to the plane
    OR
  - one vector perpendicular (or normal) to the plane

Vector equation 1:	Explanation:
$r = a + \lambda b + \mu c$ - r is position vector of any point on the plane - a is position vector of a known point $A(a_1, a_2, a_3)$ on the plane - b and c are two non-parallel vectors that are parallel to the plane - $\lambda, \mu \in R$ are two independent parameters	If the point $R(x, y, z)$ lies on a plane containing the known point $A(a_1, a_2, a_3)$ and two non-parallel vectors $b = \begin{pmatrix} b_1 \\ b_2 \\ b_3 \end{pmatrix}$ and $c = \begin{pmatrix} c_1 \\ c_2 \\ c_3 \end{pmatrix}$, then $\overrightarrow{AR}$ $= \overrightarrow{OR} - \overrightarrow{OA}$ $= \lambda b + \mu c$ $\therefore \overrightarrow{OR} = \overrightarrow{OA} + \lambda b + \mu c$
Vector equation 2:	Explanation:
$r \bullet n = a \bullet n$ - can also be written as $n \bullet (r - a) = 0$ - n is a vector normal (i.e. perpendicular) to the plane - r is position vector of any point on the plane - a is position vector of a known point $A(a_1, a_2, a_3)$ on the plane	If two non-parallel vectors that are both parallel to the plane are b and c, then the normal vector is $n = b \times c$. 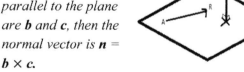 n is perpendicular to any vector in or parallel to the plane.

	If the point R(x, y, z) lies on a plane containing the known point $A(a_1, a_2, a_3)$ and which has normal vector $\mathbf{n} = \begin{pmatrix} a \\ b \\ c \end{pmatrix}$ $\overrightarrow{AR} \perp \mathbf{n} \therefore \mathbf{n} \cdot \overrightarrow{AR} = 0$ $\overrightarrow{AR} = \overrightarrow{OR} - \overrightarrow{OA} = \mathbf{r} - \mathbf{a}$ $\therefore \mathbf{n} \cdot (\mathbf{r} - \mathbf{a}) = 0$
Cartesian equation: $ax + by + cz = ax_1 + by_1 + cz_1 = d$ - d is a constant - $\mathbf{n} = \begin{pmatrix} a \\ b \\ c \end{pmatrix}$ is a normal vector to the plane - (x_1, y_1, z_1) is a point on the plane	*Explanation:* If the point R(x, y, z) lies on a plane containing the known point $A(a_1, a_2, a_3)$ and which has normal vector $\mathbf{n} = \begin{pmatrix} a \\ b \\ c \end{pmatrix}$ $\overrightarrow{AR} \perp \mathbf{n} \therefore \mathbf{n} \cdot \overrightarrow{AR} = 0$ $\therefore \begin{pmatrix} a \\ b \\ c \end{pmatrix} \cdot \begin{pmatrix} x - x_1 \\ y - y_1 \\ z - z_1 \end{pmatrix} = 0$ $a(x - x_1) + b(y - y_1) + c(z - z_1) = 0$ $\therefore ax + by + cz = ax_1 + by_1 + cz_1$ (RHS is constant)

Angles in space

	Explanation
Angle between a line and a plane	If a line with direction vector $\mathbf{d}$ intersects the normal vector $\mathbf{n}$ of a plane, the line makes an angle θ with $\mathbf{n}$ $\therefore$ from the diagram, the acute angle between the line and the plane is ϕ

	$sin\Phi = cos\Theta = \frac{|n \cdot d|}{|n||d|}$ $\therefore \Phi = arcsin\left(\frac{|n \cdot d|}{|n||d|}\right)$	
Angle between two planes	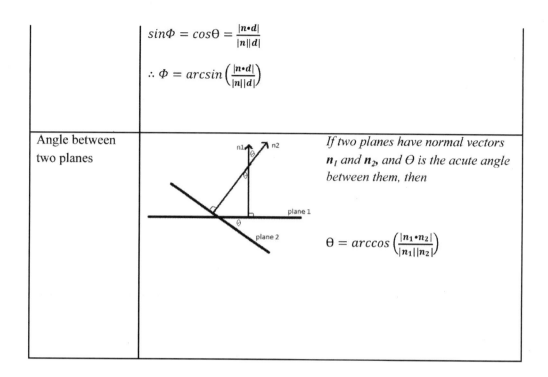	*If two planes have normal vectors n_1 and n_2, and Θ is the acute angle between them, then* $\Theta = arccos\left(\frac{|n_1 \cdot n_2|}{|n_1||n_2|}\right)$

Intersecting planes

- *arrangements of 2 planes: intersecting, parallel, coincident*
- *arrangements of 3 planes*
1. all coincident
2. 2 coincident, 1 intersecting
3. 2 coincident, 1 parallel
4. 2 parallel, 1 intersecting
5. all 3 parallel
6. all meet at one point
7. all meet in a common line
8. a line of intersecting of 2 planes is parallel to the third plane

Method	Solutions
- a general 3 X 3 system in variables x, y, and z where the coefficients of the variables are constants is $\begin{cases} a_1x + b_1y + c_1z = d_1 \\ a_2x + b_2y + c_2z = d_2 \\ a_3x + b_3y + c_3z = d_3 \end{cases}$	<u>Unique solution</u> *if $h \neq 0$, then a unique solution of 'z' can be found using $z = \frac{h}{i}$*
- augmented matrix is $\begin{pmatrix} a_1 & b_1 & c_1 | d_1 \\ a_2 & b_2 & c_2 | d_2 \\ a_3 & b_3 & c_3 | d_3 \end{pmatrix}$, which needs	*this can be used to find unique solutions of 'x' and 'y'*

be reduced by row operations to the echelon form $\begin{pmatrix} a & b & c & | & d \\ 0 & e & f & | & g \\ 0 & 0 & h & | & i \end{pmatrix}$	**No solution**
3) the echelon form can be used to solve the system, using the last row (solve $hz = i$)	if $h = 0$ and $i \neq 0$, then the last row is $0 \times z = i$, which is not possible
	∴ the system is inconsistent and there are no solutions
	Infinite solutions
	if $h = 0$ and $i = 0$, then the last row is all 0
	∴there are infinite solutions in the form
	$x = p + kt$
	$y = q + lt$
	$z = t, t \in R$

Practice time!

1. The points A (2,4,2), B (10,−2,4), C(−6,2,8) and D(10,6,14) form the vertices of a tetrahedron.

    a) Find $\vec{AC}$ and $\vec{CD}$
    b) Find the area of the triangle face ACD

2. Find a vector equation of the line passing through the points A(−6,6,14) and B(−6,2,4).

3. Find a vector equation of the line of intersection of the planes
   $9x − 3y + 3z = 48$ and $3x − 6y + 6z = 36$.

4. Find the Cartesian equation of the plane containing the line with equation
   $r = \begin{pmatrix} 3 \\ 2 \\ 2 \end{pmatrix} + \lambda \begin{pmatrix} 5 \\ 1 \\ -1 \end{pmatrix}$ and the point (2,1,4).

5. Let $p = \begin{pmatrix} 2 \\ 4 \\ 6 \end{pmatrix}$ and $q = \begin{pmatrix} 3 \\ 1 \\ 2 \end{pmatrix}$. Find $p \times q$.

6. Determine whether the lines $r = \begin{pmatrix} 4 \\ 6 \\ 8 \end{pmatrix} + t \begin{pmatrix} 2 \\ 2 \\ 0 \end{pmatrix}$ and $r = \begin{pmatrix} 10 \\ 2 \\ 6 \end{pmatrix} + s \begin{pmatrix} -0.5 \\ 5 \\ 1 \end{pmatrix}$ intersect. Find the point of intersection if they do intersect.

7. Find the shortest distance from $A(2,2,4)$ to the line $r = \begin{pmatrix} 2 \\ -4 \\ 6 \end{pmatrix} + s \begin{pmatrix} 2 \\ 4 \\ 0 \end{pmatrix}$

8. Find the angle between two unit vectors a and b if $|a + 2b| = |b − 2a|$.

9. Find the angle θ between the plane $x − 3y + 2.5z = 31.5$ and the line $\frac{x+6}{-2} = \frac{y-2}{3} = \frac{z+4}{-6}$

10. A spaceship in a videogame starts at the origin and moves with velocity $10i + 10j$ km h^{-1}. A meteor starts at $14i + 6j$ km and moves with velocity $19i − 8j$ km h^{-1}. Determine if the ship and the meteor collide. If they started at the same time.

LIMITS AND DIFFERENTIATION

Limits

- definition: let f(x) be a function defined within the interval $a - \delta < x < a + \delta$
  for every number $\varepsilon > 0$, there is a number $\delta > 0$ such that $\lim_{x \to a} f(x) = L$
  $|f(x) - L| < \varepsilon$ whenever $0 < |x - a| < \delta$

- explanation: if f(x) approaches a real number L when x approaches (**but does not equal to**) 'a', then it is said that f(x) has a limit of (or converges to) L as x approaches a
- i.e. limits describe the behavior of the function as x approaches a particular value
- a function f(x) is continuous at $x = a$ only if:
- f(a) is defined
- $\lim_{x \to a} f(x)$ exists
- $f(a) = \lim_{x \to a} f(x)$

> **Rules for Limits:** if f(x) and g(x) are functions such that $\lim_{x \to a} f(x)$ and $\lim_{x \to a} g(x)$ exist:
>
> 1. $\lim_{x \to a} c = c$
> 2. $\lim_{x \to a} cf(x) = c \lim_{x \to a} f(x)$
> 3. $\lim_{x \to a} [f(x) \pm g(x)] = \lim_{x \to a} f(x) \pm \lim_{x \to a} g(x)$
> 4. $\lim_{x \to a} [f(x) g(x)] = \lim_{x \to a} f(x) \times \lim_{x \to a} g(x)$

- methods to find limits: graphically, algebraically
- limits at infinity: limits can be used to find out behavior of functions as 'x' approaches extremely large (∞) and extremely small ($-\infty$) values
- asymptotes of graphs can be described in terms of limits (see example 3)
- trigonometric limits: if Θ is in radians, $\lim_{\theta \to 0} \frac{\sin\theta}{\theta} = 1$
- Limits is also referred to as the first principle. The general form will be provided in the data booklet

Rates of change

- rate: a ratio between changes in 2 quantities with different units e.g. $a = \frac{velocity}{time}$
- the instantaneous rate of change of a dependent variable with respect to the independent variable at a particular instant is given by the gradient of the tangent to the graph at that point

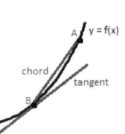

- chord (AB) – straight line joining any two points on the curve
- chord AB measures the average rate of change of f(x) over the values of 'x' from point A to B
- tangent – straight line that touches a curve at a single point
- the gradient of the tangent at point B measures the instantaneous rate of change of f(x) at point B
- as A → B, the gradient of chord AB → gradient of tangent at B
- for non-linear functions, the gradients of tangents are different at different points

"the gradient of the tangent to y = f(x) at x = a is the instantaneous rate of change in f(x) with respect to x when x = a"

Introduction to differentiation

- differentiation: the process of finding a derivative or gradient function
- the derivative function
1. represented by $f'(x)$, $\frac{dy}{dx}$, y'
2. formula: $f'(x) = \lim_{h \to 0} \frac{f(x+h)-f(x)}{h}$
3. 'h' is a small change in the value of 'x', so it can be replaced by δx
4. $f'(x) = \lim_{\delta x \to 0} \frac{\delta y}{\delta x} = \frac{dy}{dx}$ reads as 'the derivative of y with respect to x'
5. $f'(a) = \lim_{h \to 0} \frac{f(a+h)-f(a)}{h}$ gives the gradient of the tangent to $y = f(x)$ at $x = a$

- differentiation from first principles: evaluating the limit $\lim_{h \to 0} \frac{f(x+h)-f(x)}{h}$ to find a derivative function

Let $y = f(x)$ have a point $A(x, f(x))$ and $B(x+h, f(x+h))$

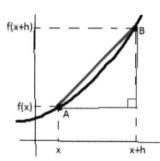

gradient of chord $AB = \frac{f(x+h)-f(x)}{x+h-x} = \frac{f(x+h)-f(x)}{h}$

as $B \to A$, gradient of $AB \to$ gradient of tangent at A

$\therefore$ gradient of tangent at any point $(x, f(x))$ is the limiting value of $\frac{f(x+h)-f(x)}{h}$ as $h \to 0$ i.e. $\lim_{h \to 0} \frac{f(x+h)-f(x)}{h}$

Rules of differentiation

Rule	f(x)	f'(x)	Proof
Differentiating a constant	$f(x) = c$	$f'(x) = 0$	
Power rule	$f(x) = x^n$	$f'(x) = nx^{n-1}$	

Scalar multiplication rule	$f(x) = cu(x)$	$f'(x) = cu'(x)$	let $f(x) = cu(x)$, c is a constant $$f'(x) = \lim_{h \to 0} \frac{f(x+h)-f(x)}{h}$$ $$= \lim_{h \to 0} \frac{cu(x+h)-cu(x)}{h}$$ $$= \lim_{h \to 0} c \left[\frac{u(x+h)-u(x)}{h}\right]$$ $$= cu'(x)$$
Addition rule	$f(x) = u(x) + v(x)$	$f'(x) = u'(x) + v'(x)$	let $f(x) = u(x) + v(x)$ $$f'(x) = \lim_{h \to 0} \frac{f(x+h)-f(x)}{h}$$ $$= \lim_{h \to 0} \frac{u(x+h)-u(x)+v(x+h)-v(x)}{h}$$ $$= \lim_{h \to 0} \frac{u(x+h)-u(x)}{h} + \lim_{h \to 0} \frac{v(x+h)-v(x)}{h}$$ $$= u'(x) + v'(x)$$
Chain rule - to easily differentiate complicated functions: write them as composite functions	$y = g(u)$ where $u = f(x)$	$\frac{dy}{dx} = \frac{dy}{du} \times \frac{du}{dx}$	Let $y = g(u)$ where $u = f(x)$ For a small change in x (δx) there is a small change in u (δu) = $f(x + \delta x) - f(x)$ and a small change in y (δy) by fraction multiplication: $\frac{\delta y}{\delta x} = \frac{\delta y}{\delta u} \times \frac{\delta u}{\delta x}$ as $\delta x \to 0$, $\delta u \to 0$ $\therefore \lim_{\delta x \to 0} \frac{\delta y}{\delta x} = \lim_{\delta u \to 0} \frac{\delta y}{\delta u} \times \lim_{\delta x \to 0} \frac{\delta u}{\delta x}$
	$y = [f(x)]^n$	$\frac{dy}{dx} = n[f(x)]^{n-1} \times f'(x)$	

			$\therefore \frac{dy}{dx} = \frac{dy}{du} \times \frac{du}{dx}$
Product rule	$f(x) = u(x)v(x)$	$f'(x) = u'(x)v(x) + v'(x)u(x)$	Let $y = u(x)v(x)$. For δx, there is a corresponding δu, δv, and δy.
	$y = uv$	$\frac{dy}{dx} = v\frac{du}{dx} + u\frac{dv}{dx}$	$y = uv, \therefore y + \delta y = (u + \delta u)(v + \delta v)$ $y + \delta y = uv + (\delta u)v + u(\delta v) + \delta u \delta v$ $\delta y = (\delta u)v + u(\delta v) + \delta u \delta v$ $\frac{\delta y}{\delta x} = \left(\frac{\delta u}{\delta x}\right)v + u\left(\frac{\delta v}{\delta x}\right) + \left(\frac{\delta u}{\delta x}\right)\delta v$ as $\delta x \to 0$, $\delta v \to 0$ $\therefore \lim_{\delta x \to 0} \frac{\delta y}{\delta x} = \left(\lim_{\delta x \to 0} \frac{\delta u}{\delta x}\right)v + u\left(\lim_{\delta x \to 0} \frac{\delta v}{\delta x}\right) + 0$ $\therefore \frac{dy}{dx} = v\frac{du}{dx} \times u\frac{dv}{dx}$
Quotient rule	$f(x) = \frac{u(x)}{v(x)}$	$f'(x) = \frac{u'(x)v(x) - v'(x)u(x)}{(v(x))^2}$	Let $f(x) = \frac{u(x)}{v(x)}, \therefore u(x) = f(x)v(x)$ By product rule:
	$y = \frac{u}{v}$	$\frac{dy}{dx} = \frac{u'v - uv'}{v^2}$	$u'(x) = f'(x)v(x) + v'(x)f(x)$ $\therefore u'(x) - v'(x)f(x) = f'(x)v(x)$ $f'(x)v(x) = u'(x) - \frac{u(x)}{v(x)}v'(x)$ $f'(x)v(x) = \frac{u'(x)v(x) - u(x)v'(x)}{v(x)}$ $\therefore f'(x) = \frac{u'(x)v(x) - v'(x)u(x)}{(v(x))^2}$

Implicit differentiation

- *implicit relations*
1. relationships between 'x' and 'y' in which it is difficult or impossible to write y as a function of x
2. e.g. $y^3 + 4xy^2 - 3xy + 8 = 0$
3. since $y = f(x)$ cannot be found, the derivative function $f'(x)$ in terms of x only also cannot be found
4. however $\frac{dy}{dx}$ = the rate of change in 'y' with respect to 'x' can be found
   - *implicit differentiation*
   - step 1: differentiate both sides of the equation with respect to 'x'
   - step 2: make $\frac{dy}{dx}$ the subject of the equation

Using chain rule:
$$\frac{d}{dx}(y^n) = ny^{n-1}\frac{dy}{dx}$$

Derivatives of functions

Function	f(x)	f'(x)	Explanation
Exponential	$f(x) = b^x$ b is a positive constant, $b \neq 0$	$f'(x) = kb^x$ k is a constant = $f'(0)$	Let $f(x) = b^x$ $f'(x)$ $= \lim_{h \to 0} \frac{b^{x+h} - b^x}{h}$ $= \lim_{h \to 0} \frac{b^x(b^h - 1)}{h}$ $= b^x \left(\lim_{h \to 0} \frac{b^h - 1}{h}\right)$ $f'(0)$ $= \lim_{h \to 0} \frac{f(0+h) - f(0)}{h}$ $= \lim_{h \to 0} \frac{b^h - 1}{h}$ $\therefore f'(x) = b^x f'(0)$
	$f(x) = e^x$	$f'(x) = e^x$	<u>This is a function which is its own derivative:</u>

$\therefore f'(0) = 1$ and $f'(x) = b^x$

$f'(0) = \lim_{h \to 0} \frac{b^h - 1}{h} = 1$

$\therefore \lim_{h \to 0} b^h = \lim_{h \to 0}(1 + h)$

Let $h = \frac{1}{n}$, so as $h \to 0$, $\frac{1}{n} \to 0$ and $n \to \infty$

$\therefore \lim_{n \to \infty} b^{\frac{1}{n}}$

$= \lim_{n \to \infty} \left(1 + \frac{1}{n}\right)$

$b = \lim_{n \to \infty} \left(1 + \frac{1}{n}\right)^n = e$

so if $f(x) = e^x$ then $f'(x) = e^x$

Properties:

1. as $x \to \infty$, $y \to \infty$ very fast so $\frac{dy}{dx} \to \infty$
   i.e. the gradient of the curve increases as 'x' increases

2. as $x \to -\infty$, $y \to 0$, so $\frac{dy}{dx} \to 0$
   i.e. as 'x' becomes large and negative, f(x)

			approaches asymptote y = 0
	$y = e^{f(x)}$	$\frac{dy}{dx} = f'(x)e^{f(x)}$	Let $y = e^{f(x)} = e^u$ where $u = f(x)$ Using chain rule, $\frac{dy}{dx}$ $= \frac{dy}{du}\frac{du}{dx}$ $= e^u \frac{du}{dx}$ $= f'(x)e^{f(x)}$
	$y = a^x$, $a > 0$	$\frac{dy}{dx} = a^x \ln a$	Let $y = a^x$, $a > 0$ $y = (e^{\ln a})^x = e^{x\ln a}$ $\therefore \frac{dy}{dx}$ $= e^{x\ln a} \times \ln a$ $= a^x \ln a$
Logarithmic	$y = \ln x$	$\frac{dy}{dx} = \frac{1}{x}$	Let $y = \ln x$, $\therefore x = e^y$ Using implicit differentiation, $1 = e^y \frac{dy}{dx}$ $\therefore 1 = x\frac{dy}{dx}$ so $\frac{1}{x} = \frac{dy}{dx}$

		$\frac{dx}{} \quad f(x)$	where $u = f(x)$
			Using chain rule, $\frac{dy}{dx} = \frac{dy}{du}\frac{du}{dx}$ $\frac{dy}{dx} = \frac{1}{u}\frac{du}{dx} = \frac{f'(x)}{f(x)}$
Trigonometric (x in radians) - circular motion gives rise to sin and cos curves - e.g. if point P moves anticlockwise around the unit circle with a linear speed of 1 unit/s, it will travel through 2π radians in 2π seconds - angular velocity of P: the rate of change of θ per unit time $\left(\frac{d\theta}{dt}\right)$ - linear speed of P: the rate of change of arc length per unit time $\left(\frac{dl}{dt}\right)$	$y = sinx$	$\frac{dy}{dx} = cosx$	Let $f(x) = sinx$ Using first principles, $f'(x)$ $= \lim_{h \to 0} \frac{sin(x+h) - sin(x)}{h}$ $= \lim_{h \to 0} \frac{2cos\left(\frac{x+h+x}{2}\right)sin\left(\frac{x+h-x}{2}\right)}{h}$ $= \lim_{h \to 0} \frac{2cos\left(x+\frac{h}{2}\right)sin\left(\frac{h}{2}\right)}{h}$ $= \lim_{h \to 0} \frac{2cos\left(x+\frac{h}{2}\right)}{2} \times \frac{sin\left(\frac{h}{2}\right)}{\frac{h}{2}}$ $= cosx \times 1$ $= cosx$
	$y = cosx$	$\frac{dy}{dx} = -sinx$	$y = cosx = sin\left(\frac{\pi}{2} - x\right)$ $\therefore y = sinu \ \left(u = \frac{\pi}{2} - x\right)$ Using chain rule,

110

	$y = \tan x$	$\dfrac{dy}{dx} = \sec^2 x$	$y = \tan x = \dfrac{\sin x}{\cos x}$ Using quotient rule, $\therefore \dfrac{dy}{dx}$ $= \dfrac{\cos x \cos x - \sin x (-\sin x)}{(\cos x)^2}$ $= \dfrac{\cos^2 x + \sin^2 x}{\cos^2 x}$ $= \dfrac{1}{\cos^2 x}$ $= \sec^2 x$
	$y = \sin[f(x)]$ $y = \cos[f(x)]$ $y = \tan[f(x)]$	$\dfrac{dy}{dx} = f'(x)\cos[f(x)]$ $\dfrac{dy}{dx} = -f'(x)\sin[f(x)]$ $\dfrac{dy}{dx} = f'(x)\sec^2[f(x)]$	*Example:* $y = \sin[f(x)]$ let $u = f(x)$, so $y = \sin u$ Using chain rule, $\dfrac{dy}{dx}$ $= \cos u \times f'(x)$ $= f'(x)\cos[f(x)]$ Use the same method to get derivatives of $y = \cos[f(x)]$ and $\tan[f(x)]$

	$y = secx$ $y = cotx$	$\frac{dy}{dx} = secx\,tanx$ $\frac{dy}{dx} = -csc^2 x$	$y = \frac{1}{sinx}$ let $u = sinx$, so $y = u^{-1}$ and $\frac{du}{dx} = cosx$ Using chain rule,
			$\frac{dy}{dx}$ $= -1u^{-2}\frac{du}{dx}$ $= \frac{-1}{(sinx)^2}cosx$ $= \frac{-1}{sinx}\frac{cosx}{sinx}$ $= -cscx\,cotx$ Use the same method to get derivative of $y = secx$ and $cotx$
Inverse trigonometric	$y = arcsinx$	$\frac{dy}{dx} = \frac{1}{\sqrt{1-x^2}}$, $x \in\,]-1, 1[$	The function $sinx$ has an inverse only in the domain $x \in [-\frac{\pi}{2}, \frac{\pi}{2}]$ If $y = arcsinx$, then $x = siny$ $\therefore \frac{dx}{dy}$ $= cosy$ $= \sqrt{1 - sin^2 y}$ $= \sqrt{1 - x^2}$ Using chain rule,

			reciprocals
			$\therefore \frac{dy}{dx} = \frac{1}{\sqrt{1-x^2}}$, $x \in]-1, 1[$
	$y = \arccos x$	$\frac{dy}{dx} = \frac{-1}{\sqrt{1-x^2}}$, $x \in]-1, 1[$	similar method as for $y = \arcsin x$
	$y = \arctan x$	$\frac{dy}{dx} = \frac{1}{1+x^2}$, $x \in R$	similar method as for $y = \arcsin x$

Second and higher derivatives

- $f'(x)$ is also called the first derivative
- the second derivative
1. the derivative of $f'(x)$ / the derivative of the first derivative
2. notation: $f''(x), y''$, or $\frac{d^2y}{dx^2}$
3. $\frac{d^2y}{dx^2} = \frac{d}{dx}\left(\frac{dy}{dx}\right)$
   - nth derivative with respect to x
   - obtained by differentiating $y = f(x)$ 'n' times
     - notation: $f^n(x)$ or $\frac{d^n y}{dx^n}$

PROPERTIES OF CURVES

Property	Explanation	Graphs and Diagrams
Tangent	*concept:* if $P(a, f(a))$ is a point on the curve $y = f(x)$, the gradient of the tangent to the curve at P is $m_T = f'(a)$ *equation:* $f'(a) = \frac{y-f(a)}{x-a}$ **or** $y - f(a) = f'(a)(x-a)$	gradient = m(T) P(a, f(a))
Normal	*definition:* a line which is perpendicular to the tangent at the point of contact *formula:* gradient of the normal at $x = a$ is $m_N = \frac{-1}{f'(a)}$ (gradients of perpendicular lines are negative reciprocals of each other)	P(a, f(a)) gradient = m(N)
Increasing functions - *an increase in 'x' produces an increase in 'y'*	*concept:* Let 'S' be an interval in the domain of $y = f(x)$ - **increasing** - $f(a) \leq f(b)$ for all $a, b \in S$ such that $a < b$	decreasing increasing minimum point where derivative func = 0

Decreasing functions – *an increase in 'x' produces a decrease in 'y'*	- **decreasing** – $f(a) \geq f(b)$ for all $a, b \in S$ such that $a < b$ *using $f'(x)$:* 1. **increasing** - $f'(x) \geq 0$ for all x in S 2. **strictly increasing** - $f'(x) > 0$ for all x in S 3. **monotone increasing** – functions that are increasing for all $x \in R$ 4. **decreasing** - $f'(x) \leq 0$ for all x in S 5. **strictly decreasing** - $f'(x) < 0$ for all x in S 6. **monotone decreasing** – functions that are decreasing for all $x \in R$	monotone increasing monotone decreasing
	sign diagrams of $f'(x)$: useful for determining the intervals for which a function is increasing or decreasing step 1: find $f'(x)$ from the given function step 2: find the values of 'x' for which $f'(x) = 0$ step 3: draw a sign diagram and mark these values of 'x' step 4: substitute values of 'x' on either side of the marked values and check whether the function is increasing (+) or decreasing (-)	(graph with $x = -2$ and $x = 3$) E.g. let $f(x)$ be a function for which $f'(x) = 0$ at $x = -2$ and $x = 3$ (sign diagram: + from left to -2, − between -2 and 3, + after 3) $f(x)$ is $\begin{cases} \text{increasing for } x \leq -2 \text{ and } x \geq 3 \\ \text{decreasing for } -2 \leq x \leq 3 \end{cases}$

Stationary points	*definition*: the point(s) where $f'(x) = 0$	
	types: 1. turning points – max/min 2. stationary points of inflection *turning points:* 1. **Global minimum** – The minimum value of y in the entire domain 2. **Local minimum** – Turning point where $f'(x) = 0$ and the curve has an upward U shape 3. **Global maximum** – The maximum value of y in the entire domain 4. **Local max** – turning point where $f'(x) =$	Global minimum Global maximum
	0 *and curve has downward U shape* (local max or min can also be a global max or min e.g. quadratic graphs) *stationary points of inflection:* - a point on the graph where $f'(x) = 0$ but is neither a max nor min - there is a change in curvature/shape of graph - is not a turning point i.e. graph does not change from increasing to decreasing or vice versa	Local Maximum Local Minimum

	sign diagrams: turning points and stationary points of inflection have characteristic sign diagrams 1. **local max** – sign changes from +ve to –ve over the point where $f'(x) = 0$ 2. **local min** – sign changes from –ve to +ve over the point where $f'(x) = 0$ 3. **stationary inflection** – sign does not change over the point where $f'(x) = 0$	let $f'(a) = 0$ + | – x=a (local max) – | + x=a (local min) + | + x=a (stationary inflection) – | – x=a (stationary inflection)

Inflections and shape	*test for shapes:*
	
	1. **concave downwards**
	   - as x increases, gradient decreases
	   - $f'(x)$ is decreasing
	   - $\therefore f''(x) < 0$
	
	2. **concave upwards**
	   - as x increases, gradient increases
	   - $f'(x)$ is increasing
	   - $\therefore f''(x) > 0$
	
	points of inflection: corresponds to a change in curvature
	
	1. **stationary inflection** – tangent at the point of inflection is horizontal ($m_T = 0$)
	
	2. **non stationary inflection** – tangent at point of inflection is not horizontal
		Concave Downwards
		
		Concave Upwards
		
		Stationary point of inflection

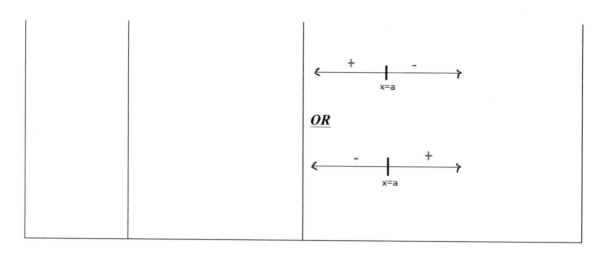

Summary: classifying stationary points

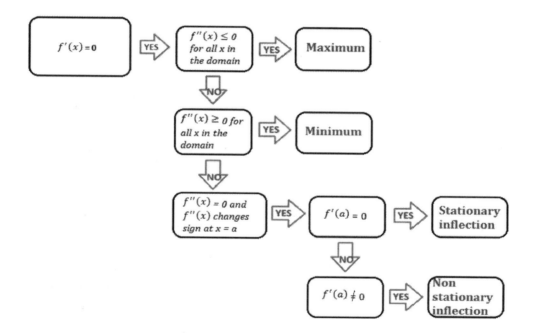

APPLICATIONS OF DIFFERENTIAL CALCULUS

Kinematics

- w.r.t motion in a straight line
- displacement (m)
1. if a particle P moves along a <u>straight line</u> from origin O, its position 's' relative to O can be described by a function of time (t)
2. ∴ **s = s(t),** t ≥ 0 *(displacement function)*
3. vector quantity - magnitude is its distance from O, direction is represented by its sign
   - velocity (ms^{-1})
   - average velocity is the change in displacement (Δs) divided by the time taken (Δt = $t_2 - t_1$)
   - formula: avg $v = \frac{s(t_2)-s(t_1)}{t_2-t_1}$
   - instantaneous velocity is the instantaneous rate of change of displacement i.e. v(t) is the derivative of s(t)
   - formula: $v(t) = s'(t) = \lim_{h \to 0} \frac{s(t+h)-s(t)}{h}$

   - acceleration (ms^{-2})
   - average acceleration is the change in velocity (Δv) divided by the time taken (Δt = $t_2 - t_1$)
   - formula: avg $a = \frac{v(t_2)-v(t_1)}{t_2-t_1}$
   - instantaneous acceleration is the instantaneous rate of change of velocity i.e. a(t) is the derivative of v(t)
   - formula:
     $a(t) = v'(t) = s''(t) = \lim_{h \to 0} \frac{v(t+h)-v(t)}{h}$
   - initial conditions: the position, velocity, and acceleration of a particle at t = 0 i.e. s(0), v(0), and a(0)
   - speed
   - magnitude of a particle's velocity i.e. S = |v|
   - represented by function S(t)

if s(t) > 0, P is to the right of O
if s(t) = 0, P is at O
if s(t) < 0, P is to the left of O

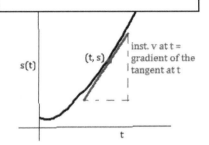

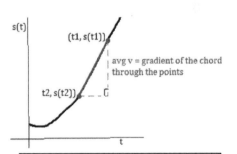

if v(t) > 0, P is moving right
if v(t) = 0, P is instantaneously at rest
if a(t) > 0, velocity is increasing
if a(t) = 0, velocity may be max, min, or constant
S is increasing if the sign of v(t) and a(t) are the same
S is decreasing of v(t) and a(t) have opposite signs

Rates of change

- concept: $\frac{dy}{dx}$ is the rate of change of y with respect to x
- can be applied to real life situations e.g. temperature variations, variations in height of tides, etc

Optimization

- definition: the process of finding the minimum or maximum value of a function
- the solution is called the 'optimum solution'
- methods: use of technology, analytical methods, differential calculus

*the max/min value may not always occur when $f'(x)$. always check given interval

1. step 1: draw a diagram of the problem
2. step 2: write a formula with one variable subject (i.e. the variable that has to be optimized) and its domain
3. step 3: find the first derivative
4. step 4: find the values of 'x' that make the first derivative 0
5. step 5: check for any global max/min within the specified domain (i.e. the endpoints of the domain, any points where the derivative is not defined)
6. step 6: use the sign diagram test, 2nd derivative test, or graphical test to classify the solutions at max/min
7. step 7: answer the question

- tests for classifying optimum solutions:

Sign diagram test: at $x = a$ where $f'(a) = 0$	Graphical test: graph the function	2nd derivative test: at $x = a$ where $f'(a) = 0$
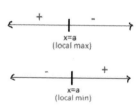	concave downward – local max concave upward – local min	if $\frac{d^2y}{dx^2} < 0$, (local max) if $\frac{d^2y}{dx^2} > 0$, (local min)

Related rates of change

- related rates problems involve differential equations where one of the variables is time (t)
- differential equations: equations that include derivatives
- solving related rates problems
- step 1: draw a diagram of the problem
- step 2: identify the variables and the constants in the problem
- step 3: construct an equation that connects the variables
- step 4: differentiate the equation with respect to time 't' to get a differential equation

example of a differential equation:

if $x^3 + y^2 = 3$, its differential equation with respect to time 't' is $3x^2\frac{dy}{dx} + 2y\frac{dy}{dt} = 0$

Practice Time!

1. Prove from first principles that the derivative of x^3 is $3x^2$.
2. Prove from first principles that the derivative of $x^2 + 3x - 2$ is $2x + 3$.
3. Check if there are values of x for which the function $f(x) = e^x \sin 3x$ has a gradient of 0.
4. Differentiate $f(x) = xy + 2y^2x^2$.
5. Find the equation of the normal to the curve $y = \ln x + 3x$ at $x = 1$
6. Find the stationary points on the curve $y = 9x^3 - 12x^2 - 11x - 2$
7. Find the smallest surface area of a base less cone with a capacity to hold $100cm^3$ of water.
8. Find the coordinates of the point of inflection on the curve $y = x^3 - 6x^2 + 3.5$
9. A bubble is floating up towards the surface of a liquid. Its radius is increasing at a rate of 3 /s . At what rate is the volume of the sphere increasing when the radius is 7 cm?
10. An object has speed v at a displacement x, linked by the equation $v = e^x \cos x + 5$. Find the acceleration in terms of the displacement.

INTEGRATION

Introduction

- involves anti-differentiation (reverse process)
- applications:

1. area under curves e.g. distance travelled in velocity graphs
2. volumes of revolution
3. economics, biology, statistics
4. solutions of differential equations

- <u>concept 1</u>: area under a curve
- example: estimate area (A) enclosed by the curve $f(x) = x^2$ and the lines $y = 0$, $x = 1$, and $x = 4$
- Step 1: subdivide the interval $1 \leq x \leq 4$ into three rectangles of width 1 unit and calculate the areas of the rectangles

Upper estimate of A	Lower estimate of A
upper rectangles (U) - top edges are at the maximum value of the curve in that rectangle 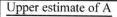 $A_U = 1 \times f(2) + 1 \times f(3) + 1 \times f(4)$ $= 4 + 9 + 16$ $= 29$ units^2	lower rectangles (L) - top edges at the minimum value of the curve in that rectangle $A_L = 1 \times f(1) + 1 \times f(2) + 1 \times f(3)$ $= 1 + 4 + 9$ $= 14$ units^2

- Step 2: realize that $A_L < A < A_U$
    $< A < 29$
- Step 3: use a smaller subdivision (e.g. a width of ½, dividing the interval $1 \leq x \leq 4$ rectangles) and calculate A_L A_U again
• Step 4: let the width of a subdivision = and use the concept of limits to calculate A_L

A_U
$= ½ [f(1.5) + f(2) + f(2.5) + f(3) + f(3.5) + f(4)]$
$= 24.875$ units²

A_L
$= ½[f(1) + f(1.5) + f(2) + f(2.5) + f(3) + f(3.5)]$
$= 17.375$ units²

∴ 14

into 6 and

and

- *concept 2: the definite integral*

1. $A = \int_a^b f(x)dx$ is called the 'definite integral of f(x) from a to b'

2. if $f(x) \geq 0$ for all $a \leq x \leq b$ then $\int_a^b f(x)dx$ = area under the curve between $x = a$ and $x = B$

Explanation	Calculation
the function f(x) has to be positive, continuous, and increasing in the interval $a \leq x \leq b$	$A_L = w[f(x_0) + f(x_1) + f(x_2) + \cdots + f(x_{n-1})]$ $= w \sum_{i=0}^{n-1} f(x_i)$
the interval is divided into 'n' subintervals, and each subinterval has a width (w) $= \frac{b-a}{n}$	$A_U = w[f(x_1) + f(x_2) + f(x_3) + \cdots + f(x_n)]$ $= w \sum_{i=1}^{n} f(x_i)$
calculate A_L and A_U	$A_U - A_L = w(f(x_n) - f(x_0))$ $= \frac{1}{n}(b-a)(f(b) - f(a))$
use the concept of limits to calculate A	$\therefore \lim_{n \to \infty}(A_U - A_L)$ as $\lim_{A_U - A_L} \frac{1}{n} = 0$
since $A_L < A < A_U$ for all n, $\lim_{n \to \infty}(A_U) = A = \lim_{n \to \infty}(A_L)$	$\therefore \lim_{n \to \infty}(A_U) = \lim_{n \to \infty}(A_L)$

- *concept 3: anti-differentiation*

  - the process of finding y from $\frac{dy}{dx}$ or f(x) from $f'(x)$

  - also called integration

  - integrating power functions – index should increase by 1 (as it decreases by 1 during differentiation)

> *if F(x) is a function where $F'(x) = f(x)$,*
>
> *derivative of F(x) is f(x)*

however, $\frac{dy}{dx} = x^2$ for $y = \frac{1}{3}x^3, \frac{1}{3}x^3 + 1, \frac{1}{3}x^3 + 2, \ldots$

i.e. if $y = \frac{1}{3}x^3 + c$, then $\frac{dy}{dx} = x^2$

Indefinite Integrals

- integration that is not applied to a specific interval
- if $F'(x) = f(x)$, then $\int f(x)dx = F(x) + c$
- arbitrary or integrating constant 'c' $\in R$
- rules:

1. any constant can be written in front of the integral sign

$$\int kf(x)dx = k\int f(x)dx$$

2. the integral of a sum is the sum of the individual integrals

$$\int f(x) + g(x)dx = \int f(x)dx + \int g(x)dx$$

3. the value of constant 'c' can be found if the question gives a particular value of the function

e.g. let $f'(x) = 2x - 1$ and $f(0) = 3$

$$f(x) = \int 2x - 1 dx = x^2 - x + c$$

$$f(0) = c = 3 \therefore f(x) = x^2 - x + 3$$

Function	Integral
K	$kx + c$
x^n	$\dfrac{x^{n+1}}{n+1} + c, n \neq -1$
$(ax+b)^n$	$\dfrac{1}{a}\dfrac{(ax+b)^{n+1}}{n+1} + c, n \neq 1$
e^x	$e^x + c$
$\dfrac{1}{x}$	$\ln|x| + c$
e^{ax+b}	$\dfrac{1}{a}e^{ax+b} + c, a \neq 0$
$\dfrac{1}{ax+b}$	$\dfrac{1}{a}\ln|ax+b| + c, a \neq 0$
$\cos x$	$\sin x + c$
$\sin x$	$-\cos x + c$
$\sec^2 x$	$\tan x + c$

*check whether your integration is correct by differentiating your answer

Types of Integration

Type	Explanation
Integrating trigonometric functions	Type 1: cosx - $\int \cos x \, dx = \sin x + c$ - $\int \sin x \, dx = -\cos x + c$ - $\int \sec^2 x \, dx = \tan x + c$ Type 2: $\cos(ax+b)$

	1. $\int \cos(ax+b)\,dx = \frac{1}{a}\sin(ax+b) + c, a \neq 0$ 2. $\int \sin(ax+b)\,dx = -\frac{1}{a}\cos(ax+b) + c, a \neq 0$ 3. $\int \sec^2(ax+b)\,dx = \frac{1}{a}\tan(ax+b) + c, a \neq 0$ *Type 3: $\sin^2(ax+b)$ and $\cos^2(ax+b)$* - use the identities $\sin^2\theta = \frac{1}{2} - \frac{1}{2}\cos(2\theta)$ or $\cos^2\theta = \frac{1}{2} + \frac{1}{2}\cos(2\theta)$ to substitute for $\sin^2(ax+b)$ or $\cos^2(ax+b)$ in the integral - then solve using the same method as for type 2
Integration by substitution – to integrate functions that are the product of 2 expressions	$\int f(u)\frac{du}{dx}\,dx = \int f(u)\,du$ - *Proof:* Let $F(u)$ be the anti-derivative of $f(u)$ $\therefore \frac{dF}{du} = f(u)$, $\int f(u)\,du = F(u) + c$ By chain rule, $\frac{dF}{dx} = \frac{dF}{du}\frac{du}{dx} = f(u)\frac{du}{dx}$ $\therefore \int f(u)\frac{du}{dx}\,dx = F(u) + c = \int f(u)\,du$ - *Examples of possible substitutions:* 1. $u = f(x)$ for functions with $\sqrt{f(x)}$ 2. $u = \ln x$ for functions with $\ln x$ 3. $x = a\sin\theta$ for functions with $\sqrt{a^2 - x^2}$ 4. $x = a\tan\theta$ or functions with $x^2 + a^2$ or $\sqrt{x^2 + a^2}$ 5. $x = a\sec\theta$ for functions with $\sqrt{x^2 - a^2}$

Integration by parts – to integrate a function that is written as a product	$\int uv'\,dx = uv - \int vu'$
	- comes from product rule of differentiation - 'u' should be easy to differentiate and 'v' should be easy to integrate - method may need to be used twice to find an integral

Definite Integrals

$$\int_a^b f(x)\,dx = [F(x)]_a^b = F(b) - F(a)$$

1. ref. to the fundamental theorem of calculus and properties of definite integrals above
2. $\int_a^b f(x)\,dx$ is the integral from a to b of f(x) with respect to x
3. called 'definite' because the lower and upper limits of the integration are given (i.e. a
4. and b)
5. results in a numerical answer
6. the integrating constant 'c' is omitted as it will cancel out while solving the integral (i.e. through subtraction)

APPLICATIONS OF INTEGRATION

Area under a curve

- if f(x) is positive and continuous on the interval $a \leq x \leq b$, then the area (A) bounded by y = f(x) and the lines y = 0, x = a, and x = b is

$$A = \int_a^b f(x)\,dx$$

- if f(y) is positive and continuous on the interval $a \leq y \leq b$, then the area (A) bounded by x = f(y) and the lines x = 0, y = a, and y = b is

$$A = \int_a^b f(y)\,dy$$

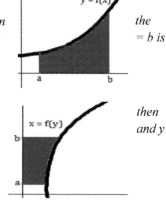

Area between two functions

1. if two functions f(x) and g(x) intersect at x = a and x = b, and g(x) for all a ≤ x ≤ b, the area (A) of the shaded region between points of intersection is

$$A = \int_a^b [f(x) - g(x)]dx$$

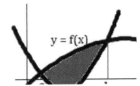

*this property can also be used when there is more than 1 quadrant contained between f(x) and g(x)

f(x) ≥ their

2. if y = f(x) = 0, then the enclosed area is

$$A = \int_a^b [-g(x)]dx = -\int_a^b g(x)dx$$

Kinematics (linear motion)

3. if a velocity time function v(t) is ≥ 0 in the interval $t_1 \leq t \leq t_2$, then the distance (d) travelled is

$$d = \int_{t_1}^{t_2} v(t)dt$$

4. if a velocity time function v(t) is ≤ 0 in the interval $t_1 \leq t \leq t_2$, then the distance (d) travelled is

$$d = -\int_{t_1}^{t_2} v(t)dt$$

Basics:
- $s(t) = \int v(t)dt$

5. the change in displacement (s) in the time interval $t_1 \leq t \leq t_2$ is

$$s = s(t_2) - s(t_1) = \int_{t_1}^{t_2} v(t)dt$$

6. total distance travelled (d_T) in the time interval $t_1 \leq t \leq t_2$ for a velocity function v(t) = s'(t) is

$$d_T = \int_{t_1}^{t_2} |v(t)|dt$$

Calculating total distance travelled:

- draw a sign diagram for v(t) to determine changes in direction
- determine s(t) by integration, including the constant 'c'
- find $s(t_1)$ and $s(t_2)$
- find s(t) at each time the direction changes
- draw a motion diagram and

Solids of revolution

7. a 3-D solid that is formed when

- the shaded area between y = f(x) and y = 0 for a ≤ x ≤ b is revolved about the x-axis through 2π (360°)

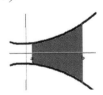

- the shaded area between x = f(y) and x = 0 for a ≤ y ≤ b is revolved about the y-axis through 2π (360°)

- volume of revolution (V)
    - integration can be used to find the volume of the solid of revolution between $x = a$ and $x = b$
    - $V = \pi \int_a^b y^2 dx$ **OR** $V = \pi \int_a^b x^2 dy$
- volumes for 2 defining functions
    - a region is bounded by an upper function $y_U = f(x)$, a lower function $y_L = g(x)$, and the lines $x = a$ and $x = b$
    - if this region is revolved about the x-axis, its volume of revolution is

$$V = \pi \int_a^b ([f(x)]^2 - [g(x)]^2)\, dx$$

Volume formula:

The solid of revolution can be made up by an infinite number of cylindrical discs.

V (cylinder) $= \pi r^2 h$

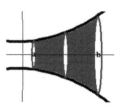

V (leftmost disc) $= \pi[f(a)]^2 h$

V (rightmost disc) $= \pi[f(b)]^2 h$

V (middle disc) $= \pi[f(x)]^2 h$

there are infinite discs, so $h \to 0$

Practise time!

1. Let $f(u) = u^{\frac{2}{3}}\left(3 - \dfrac{1}{2u^{\frac{4}{3}}}\right)$. Find $\int f(t)dt$.

2. Using the substitution $u = a - x$, or otherwise, find
$$\int \left(\dfrac{x - \dfrac{a}{2}}{a - x}\right)^2 dx.$$

3. Find $\int \lambda \sin \lambda x . e^{\lambda x} dx$.

4. Find $\int \dfrac{1}{(x-2)^2 .(x+1)} dx$.

5. Find $\int \dfrac{(\ln x)^2}{x} dx$.

6. By suitable substitution find $\int \dfrac{1}{\sqrt{2x - x^2}} dx.$

7. Find the area enclosed by the curves $y = \dfrac{1}{1+x^2}$ and $y = e^x$, $x = 0$ and $x = 1$.
Find the volume generated by revolving the enclosed area around x-axis for $\dfrac{\pi}{2}$ radians.

8. Find the total area enclosed by the curves $y = x^2 - 5x + 6$ and $y = x + 1$.

9. Given that $f(x) = \sin x$, $0 \le x \le \dfrac{3\pi}{2}$, find the volume of the solid formed when the graph of f is rotated through 2π radians about the x-axis.

10. Find the area of the region completely enclosed by the curve $y = e^{x-1} + x - 2$ and the coordinate axes.

Statistics and Probability

Measures of Central Tendency

- Mean - $\mu = \dfrac{\sum_{i=1}^{k} f_i x_i}{N}$, where $N = \sum_{i=1}^{k} f_i$. k represents the number of groups (or intervals).

- Median is the middle number when the data is ordered. If number of observations n is odd, then median is $\left(\dfrac{n+1}{2}\right)th$ number. If n is even, then median is average of $\dfrac{n}{2}th$ and $\left(\dfrac{n}{2}+1\right)th$ numbers.

- Mode is the most frequent data or class of data.

Measures of Spread

Variance of a population $\sigma^2 = \dfrac{\sum_{i=1}^{k}(x_i - \mu)^2}{N} = \dfrac{\sum_{i=1}^{k} f_i(x_i - \mu)^2}{N} = \dfrac{1}{N}\sum_{i=1}^{k} f_i x_i^2 - \mu^2$

Standard Deviation of a population $\sigma = \sqrt{\dfrac{\sum_{i=1}^{k} f_i(x_i - \mu)^2}{N}}$

Sample Variance or Unbiased estimate of the population Variance $s_{n-1}^2 = \dfrac{\sum_{i=1}^{k} f_i(x_i - \mu)^2}{N-1}$

Interquartile Range

1. Find median of entire data set.
2. Find median of the lower half of the data set. It's called lower quartile.
3. Find median of the upper half of the data set. It's called upper quartile.

    IQR (Interquartile Range) = Upper Quartile − Lower Quartile

    Box Plots or Box-and-whisker Plots

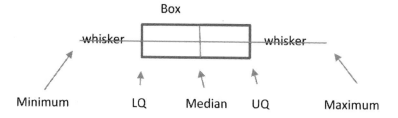

Probability

Theoretical Probability = $\dfrac{No.\ of\ favorable\ outcomes}{Total\ No.\ of\ possible\ outcomes}$

Experimental Probability = $\dfrac{No.\ of\ times\ desired\ event\ occurs}{total\ no.\ of\ trials}$

$0 \le P \le 1$

Mutually Exclusive Events

Two events A and B are said to be mutually exclusive (or disjoint) if they have no elements in common,

$A \cap B = \varnothing$.

$P(A \cup B) = P(A) + P(B)$

Complementary Events

Complement of an event is the event not occurring.

$P' = 1 - P$; $P(A') = 1 - P(A)$

Complement of an event A can also be written as A^c or $\overline{A}$ instead of A'.

Venn Diagrams

Complement of Event A is A'

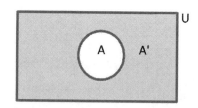

Intersection of A and B: A ∩ B

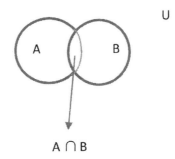

A ∩ B

Union of A and B: A ∪ B

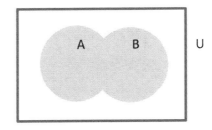

Conditional Probability

Probability of event A given that event B has already occurred,

$$P(A|B) = \frac{P(A \cap B)}{P(B)}, P(B) \neq 0.$$

Similarly, $P(B|A) = \frac{P(A \cap B)}{P(A)}, P(A) \neq 0.$

Independent Events

Events A and B are said to be independent of each other if occurrence of one event doesn't affect the other event.

Events A and B are independent if $P(A \cap B) = P(A) \times P(B)$.

Bayes' Theorem

- Law of Total Probability: $P(A) = P(A \cap B) + P(A \cap B')$

- Bayes' Theorem for Two events:

$$P(A|B) = \frac{P(A \cap B)}{P(B)} = \frac{P(A) \times P(B|A)}{P(A) \times P(B|A) + P(A') \times P(B|A')}$$

- Bayes' theorem for Three events:

$$P(A_1|B) = \frac{P(A_1 \cap B)}{P(B)} = \frac{P(B|A_1) \times P(A_1)}{P(B|A_1) \times P(A_1) + P(B|A_2) \times P(A_2) + P(B|A_3) \times P(A_3)}$$

Discrete Random Variables

A discrete random variable can take exactly n numerical values. Each of the numerical values correspond to one of the events in the sample space.

Properties:

- $0 \leq P(X = x_i) \leq 1$

- For n mutually exclusive and exhaustive events $A_1, A_2, ..., A_n$ of the sample space S, the sum of corresponding probabilities must be 1.

$$\sum_{i=1}^{i=n} P(X = x_i) = P(X = x_1) + P(X = x_2) + ... + P(X = x_n) = 1$$

where $P(X = x_i)$ is the probability of event A_i occurring.

Expectation of Discrete Random Variables

Expected value of X, $E(X) = \sum_{i=1}^{i=n} x_i P(X = x_i)$

$$= x_1 \times P(X = x_1) + x_2 \times P(X = x_2) + ... + x_n \times P(X = x_n)$$

Properties:

1. $E(a) = a$, where a is a constant.

2. $E(aX) = a.E(X)$, where a is a constant.

3. $E(f(X)) = \sum_{i=1}^{i=n} f(x_i) \times P(X = x_i)$

4. $E(aX+b) = \sum_{i=1}^{i=n} (ax_i + b) \times P(X = x_i) = aE(X) + b$

Variance of Discrete Random Variables

Variance, $\text{Var}(X) = E((X-\mu)^2) = \sum_{i=1}^{i=n} (x - \mu)^2 P(X = x)$

$\text{Var}(X) = E(X^2) - (E(X))^2 = E(X^2) - \mu^2$

Properties:

Binomial Distribution

Bernoulli Trials: An experiment in which a single action is repeated many times identically. There are only two possible outcomes of the action. For example, flipping a coin several times in identical manner is a case of Bernoulli trials. The outcome of flipping a coin can be either 'heads' or 'tails'. The outcomes can also be defined as 'success' or 'failure'.

$$P(X=x) = \binom{n}{x} p^x q^{n-x} = \binom{n}{x} p^x (1-p)^{n-x}, \quad x = 0, 1, 2, \ldots, n$$

Binomial distribution is represented as $X \sim B(n, p)$, where n is the number of trials and p is probability of success.

Expectation, Mode and Variance for the binomial distribution

Expectation $\mu = E(X) = np$

Mode of X is the value of x with the largest probability

Variance $Var(X) = npq = np(1-p)$.

Hypergeometric Distribution

Representation $X \sim Hg(n, D, N)$

where N is the size of Population

D is number of defective items

n is size of random sample selected without replacement

X is a random variable defined as the number of defectives observed in the sample of size n

$$P(X=x) = \frac{\binom{D}{x} \times \binom{N-D}{n-x}}{\binom{N}{n}}, \quad x = 0, 1, 2, \ldots, n.$$

Mean and Variance of the hypergeometric distribution

$$\mu = E(X) = \frac{nD}{N}$$

$$\sigma^2 = Var(X) = \frac{nD(N-D)(N-n)}{N^2(N-1)}$$

Poisson Distribution

An event is equally likely to occur in any given time interval.

The occurrence of an event at a point of time is independent of when other events have occurred.

Expected number of events in a given time interval is proportional to the size of the time interval.

X(t) is the number of events in a time interval of length t. Rate of random process is λ per unit time.

$X(t) \sim Pn(\lambda t)$

$\mu = \lambda t$

$$P(X=x) = \frac{e^{-\mu}\mu^x}{x!}, x = 0, 1, 2, 3, \ldots,$$

Poisson Recurrence Formula

$$P(X = x+1) = \frac{\mu}{x+1} P(X = x), x = 0, 1, 2, \ldots$$

Mean and Variance of the Poisson Distribution

$E(X) = Var(X) = \mu$

Normal Distribution

For standard normal curve, $\mu = 0, \sigma = 1$.

$$f(z) = \frac{1}{\sqrt{2\pi}} e^{-\frac{z^2}{2}}, -\infty < z < \infty$$

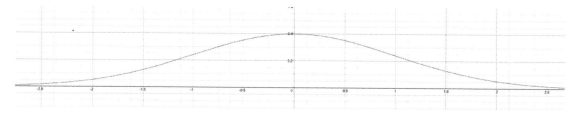

The curve is called bell-shaped curve. Total area under the curve is 1.

$X \sim N(\mu, \sigma^2)$, X is normally distributed random variable with mean μ and variance σ^2.

$$\text{Probability density function } f(x) = \frac{1}{\sigma\sqrt{2\pi}} e^{-\frac{1}{2}\left(\frac{x-\mu}{\sigma}\right)^2}$$

Properties:

- Curve is symmetrical about $x = \mu$ line.
- Mode occurs at $x = \mu$.
- x-axis is horizontal asymptote of the curve.
- Area under the curve is 1.
- $\mu - 2\sigma \leq x \leq \mu + 2\sigma$ contains 95% of the data.
- $p(a \leq X \leq b) = \int_a^b f(x)dx = \int_a^b \frac{1}{\sigma\sqrt{2\pi}} e^{-\frac{1}{2}\left(\frac{x-\mu}{\sigma}\right)^2} dx$

Converting a Normal Distribution into Standard Normal Distribution:

Use transformation $Z = \frac{X - \mu}{\sigma}, Z \sim N(0, 1)$

How to Calculate Probabilities:

$P(Z < a) = \Phi(a)$

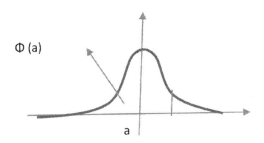

$\Phi(a)$

$P(Z > a) = 1 - P(Z < a) = 1 - \Phi(a)$

$P(Z < -a) = P(Z > a) = 1 - \Phi(a)$

$P(Z > -a) = P(Z < a) = \Phi(a)$

$P(a < Z < b) = P(Z < b) - P(Z < a) = \Phi(b) - \Phi(a)$

Calculating Quantiles or Percentiles:

It means to find value of 'a' for which $P(X \leq a) = p$, where p is the pth percentile.

$P(X \leq a) = p \Leftrightarrow P(Z \leq \frac{a - \mu}{\sigma}) = p, 0 \leq p \leq 1$

$\Rightarrow \frac{a - \mu}{\sigma} = \Phi^{-1}(p)$ where Φ^{-1} is the reading we get from Inverse Cumulative Normal Distribution table

Practice time!

1. A machine produces packets of salt. The weights in grams of 40 packets chosen at random are shown below.

Weight (g)	49.9	49.8	49.6	50.0	50.1	50.2	50.3
Frequency	7	6	4	8	6	5	4

   Find unbiased estimates of
   (a) the mean of the population from which this sample is taken;
   (b) the variance of the population from which this sample is taken.

2. Find interquartile range for sample of data 65, 69, 56, 45, 89, 12, 46, 78, 32, 65, 79, 46, 13, 64, 94, 34, 61, 94, 61, 78, 14, 45, 79, 25, 47, 68, 27, 47.

3. Given that $P(X) = \frac{1}{3}$, $P(Y|X) = \frac{1}{5}$, $P(Y|X') = \frac{1}{4}$, find $P(Y')$ and $P(X' \cup Y')$.

4. Bag 1 contains 3 red cubes and 4 black cubes. Bag 2 contains 5 red cubes and 3 black cubes. Two cubes are drawn at random, the first from bag 1 and the second from bag 2.
   (a) Find the probability that the cubes are of same color.
   (b) Given that the cubes selected are of different colors, find the probability that the red cube was selected from bag 1.

5. A boy plays a game to win prizes. The probability that he wins a prize is $\frac{1}{5}$. He plays the game 10 times. X denotes number of prizes that he wins.
   (a) E(X);
   (b) $P(X \leq 2)$.

6. Casualties arrive at an accident unit with a mean rate of two every 15 minutes. Assume that number of arrivals can be modelled by a Poisson distribution.
   (a) Find the probability that there are no arrivals in a given one hour time period.
   (b) A nurse works for three hours. Find the probability that fewer than 15 casualties arrived in this period.

7. A continuous random variable X has probability density function
$$f(x) = \frac{2}{\pi\sqrt{1-x^2}}, 0 \leq x \leq 1$$
$$= 0, \quad \text{elsewhere}$$
   Find E(X).

8. The random variable X is normally distributed and
   $P(X \leq 4) = 0.573$
   $P(X \leq 6) = 0.836$

Find E(X).
9. A continuous random variable, X, has probability density function

   $f(x) = \cos x, \ 0 \le x \le \dfrac{\pi}{2}$.

   Find the median of X.
10. The mass of new born puppies may be assumed normally distributed with mean 125 g and standard deviation 26 g. Given that 40% of the masses lie between 125 g and x g, where x > 125, find the value of x.

Answers

Sequence and Series

1. 0.75
2. 47
3. a. 4+5n   b. 12002
4. 11
5. $a = 1 \quad r = 3$
6. $x \geq 0$
7. 518.125
8. 48.55
9. 14
10. 20
11. a. $ 3874.06   b. $3867.41
12. $15341.52

Quadratic Equations:

1. a. $3, -2$ b. $4, -1$ c. $8, -3$ d. $6, -3$
2. a. $(0.875, -6.25)$ b. $(2.25, -6.13)$ c. $(0.92, 29.96)$ d. $(0.53, -0.267)$
3. $-12 < m < 12$
4. $u = 32.14$
5.

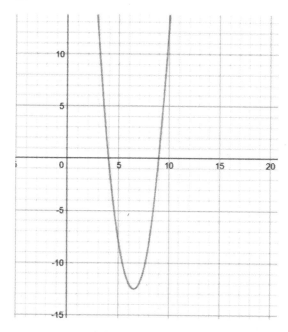

6. a. $x = -0.33$ b. $(-0.33, -8.33)$ c. x intercepts $(-2,0), (1.33,0)$
   y intercepts $(0, -8)$

d.

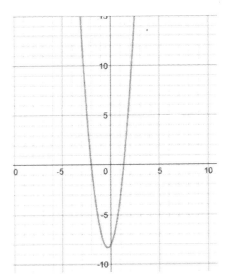

7. $t < -0.45$
8. a. $-2 < x < 5$ b. $x < 1, x > \frac{3}{2}$ c. $x \leq 0, x \geq 4$ d. $-3 \leq x \leq \frac{-1}{7}$
9. 0.125
10. $-4\sqrt{6} < n < 4\sqrt{6}$

Counting Principles

1. a. 5.839×10^{20} b. 387600
2. a. 330 b. 28
3. 1247400
4. 302400
5. 32
6. 9
7. 78
8. a. 540 b. 5400 c. 108
9. 135
10. 151200
11. 24310
12. 118755
13. 105
14. 6750
15. 308

Binomial Expansion

1. $x^8 - 8x^5 + 24x^3 - \frac{32}{x} + \frac{16}{x^4}$
2. $n = 6$ $a = \frac{1}{3}$
3. 2
4. $28x^4$

5. $160x^3$
6. 70
7. $\frac{-252}{x^5}$
8. 22400
9. $1120x^4$
10. 189190144
11. -960
12. -108864
13. *third term* (24)
14. -672
15. *not possible*
16. 145152
17. 18564
18. 6 and 7th term (489888)
19. $n = 4 \qquad k = 216$

Polynomials :

1. 0
2. $x^3 - 21x + 20$
3. $x = 1, 2$
4. $u = 3 \quad k = 33 \quad m = -10$
5. $a = 0 \quad b = -8$
6. 581
7.

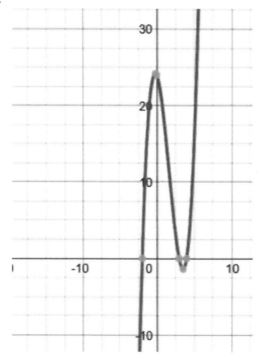

9. a. $x \geq 3$ \qquad b. $x < 2, -1 < x < 3$ \qquad c. $x \leq -7, -4 \leq x \leq 5$

10.

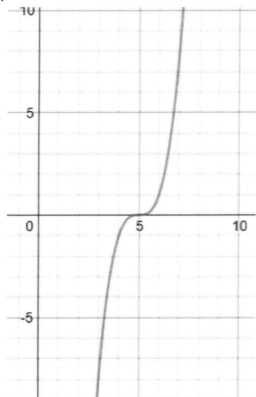

Complex Numbers

1. a. $2 - 3i$ b. $-4 + 7i$ c. 5
2. $\frac{-13}{29} + \frac{11i}{29}$
3. a. 6.403 b. 7.615
4. argand diagram drawn
5. $\sqrt{3}cis(0.955)$
6. $\frac{25\pi}{9}$
7. $-47 + 8\sqrt{3}i$
8. $6^n \left(\cos \frac{2n\pi}{5} \right)$
9. $x - \left(\frac{-3}{2} + \frac{\sqrt{11}}{2}i \right), x - \left(\frac{-3}{2} - \frac{\sqrt{11}}{2}i \right)$
10. $(x + 2)(x - i)(x + i)$

Circular Functions and Trigonometry

2. 8.576 cm^2

3. 1.4789

4.

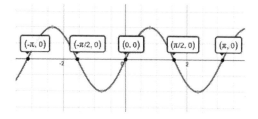

5. 0.215 , 1.88 , 2.309 , 3.974, 4.403 , 6.069

6. 0.5

7. 6.06 cm

8. $\sqrt{\dfrac{1}{t^2} - 1}$

10.

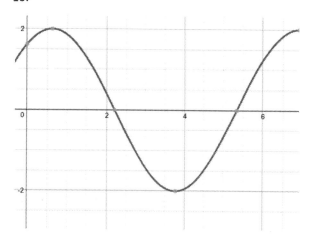

Functions-

1. a. $\left[\dfrac{3}{2}, 2\right) \cup \left(2, \dfrac{5}{2}\right]$ b. $y \geq 0$
2. $f^{-1}(x) = \dfrac{4x+2}{3-2x}$ domain - $R - \left\{\dfrac{3}{2}\right\}$
3. a. $a = -2.225$ $b = 0.225$ b. $y \geq 0$
4. $\dfrac{\ln 7}{\ln 5}$
5. $[-3, 0]$
6. 8.292
7. -0.9527
8. $x^3 - 4x^2 + x + 6$
9. a. $2 \times (x-1)^2 + 5$ b. $f(x-1) + 5$
10. $(-2, 2)$

Vectors

1. a. $\overrightarrow{AC} = \begin{pmatrix} -8 \\ -2 \\ 6 \end{pmatrix}$ $\overrightarrow{CD} = \begin{pmatrix} 16 \\ 4 \\ 6 \end{pmatrix}$ b. 74.22

2. $\vec{r} = \begin{pmatrix} -6 \\ 6 \\ 14 \end{pmatrix} + \lambda \begin{pmatrix} 0 \\ -4 \\ -10 \end{pmatrix}$

3. $\vec{r} = \begin{pmatrix} 4 \\ 0 \\ 4 \end{pmatrix} + \lambda \begin{pmatrix} 0 \\ 1 \\ 1 \end{pmatrix}$

4. $x - 9y - 4z + 23 = 0$

5. $\begin{pmatrix} 2 \\ 14 \\ -10 \end{pmatrix}$

6. They don't intersect
7. 3.35
8. $\theta = 90°$
9. 67.13°
10. They never collide

Limits and Differentiation

4. $y + x\frac{dy}{dx} + 4x^2 y + 4yx^2 \frac{dy}{dx}$

5. $y = \frac{-x+13}{4}$

6. $\left(\frac{-1}{3}, 0\right)$ $(1.22, -16.938)$

7. $90.23\ cm^2$

8. $(2, -12.5)$

9. $588\pi\ cm^3/s$

10. $e^x(\cos x - \sin x)$

Integration

1. $\frac{9u^{\frac{5}{3}}}{5} - \frac{3u^{\frac{1}{3}}}{2}$

2. $a \ln(|x-a|) - \frac{a^2}{4(x-a)} + x + C$

3. $\frac{e^{\lambda x}(\sin \lambda x - \cos \lambda x)}{2} + C$

4. $\frac{\ln(|x+1|)}{9} - \frac{\ln(|x-2|)}{9} - \frac{1}{3x-6} + C$

5. $\frac{(lnx)^3}{3} + C$

6. $\arcsin(x-1) + C$

7. $area = 0.93\ unit^2$
   $volume = 2\ unit^3$

8. $\frac{32}{3}\ unit^2$

9. $7.401\ unit^3$

10. $0.867\ unit^2$

Statistics and Probability

1. *a.* 49.9825   *b.* 0.03994
2. 34
3. $\frac{23}{30}, \frac{14}{15}$
4. *a.* $\frac{27}{56}$ *b.* $\frac{9}{29}$
5. *a.* 2   *b.* 0.6778
6. a. 0.000335   b. 0.0198
7. $\frac{2}{\pi}$
8. 3.537
9. 0.5236
10. 158.3203

Made in the USA
Middletown, DE
23 April 2018